DIN NER

The Irish Times Selection

DINNER

THE IRISH TIMES SELECTION

DOMINI KEMP

GILL & MACMILLAN

Gill & Macmillan
Hume Avenue
Park West
Dublin 12
www.gillmacmillanbooks.ie

© Domini Kemp, 2014

978 07171 6229 1

Design by www.grahamthew.com
Food photography by Frank Miller, David Sleator,
Alan Betson, Bryan O'Brien, Dara Mac Dónaill, Eric Luke,
Brenda Fitzsimmons, Cyril Byrne and Aidan Crawley
Author photo on p. viii by Barry McCall
Chapter opener artwork © Printwork/Toni Point
Indexed by Adam Pozner
Printed by Printer Trento Srl, Italy

This book is typeset in 10.5pt Onserif on 12.6pt.

acknowledgements

There are always so many people to thank and you all know who you are and how much I owe you!

Thank you first and foremost to the fantastic Orna Mulcahy, editor of the *Irish Times Magazine*, and to all my wonderful colleagues in the paper, including Marie-Claire Digby, Diarmuid Collins and Rachel Collins. Without the *Irish Times*, there would be no book!

Thank you to all the amazing *Irish Times* photographers who I have had the pleasure to work with over the years: Frank Miller, David Sleator, Alan Betson, Bryan O'Brien, Dara Mac Dónaill, Eric Luke, Brenda Fitzsimmons, Cyril Byrne and Aidan Crawley. Without your extraordinary 'eyes', my food would be ordinary!

A huge thanks to all the folk in Gill & Macmillan: Nicki Howard, Deirdre Nolan, Catherine Gough and Teresa Daly, and to the inside-outsiders Graham Thew and Nora Mahony.

Thanks to Gillian Fallon for her unwavering support and never-ending chopping, washing-up and recipe-testing throughout the last year. I hope you enjoyed the cooking, the chats and the leftovers!

And, of course, thanks to my best pals Caroline and Aisling, who have tasted my food, encouraged me and, most importantly, never let me forget the failures!

Special thanks to my sister, partner and best friend Peaches: thank you for being there with me every step of the way – through thick and thin. You know what I mean, Peachy! Thanks to my husband Garvan for being my husband (obviously), but also for being a fantastic editor, for being 'you' and for carrying us when we needed carrying. Thank you!

And to the two people I enjoy cooking for and eating with the most, without whom none of this would be worthwhile or fun: Lauren and Maeve! Best girls!

Contents
Foreword xi
Introduction xii

Lamb

Pork

foreword

I can't take credit for discovering Domini Kemp as a food writer, for it was my predecessor, Patsey Murphy, who took Domini on to write a regular column for the *Irish Times Magazine*. But I do remember Patsey's delight at having sealed the deal. It was a coup for the magazine to have this powerhouse of a woman, who had brought bagels to Ireland, could run a string of cafés in her spare time, write about the Dublin restaurant scene and operate a commercial kitchen that catered for parties. Now she would be writing recipes and styling the food photography for a new kind of column that would take the fuss out of food by creating healthy, crowd-pleasing dishes for family and friends.

Casual lunches, brunches, a supper for the in-laws, an evening with the girls, a storming Sunday dinner – Domini had the solution, while also leading readers through the food revolution that was happening on TV and in the grocery aisles. Inspired by trends coming out of New York, London, Italy and the Middle East, Domini keeps readers on their toes with new ingredients and new methods, while also suggesting healthier options to replace the holy trinity of butter, sugar and flour. Often with a Domini recipe, you don't know quite where it is going to begin. The ingredients may throw you a little – avocado instead of butter for a cake, nuts doing the work of meat, salads that call for more fruit than vegetables. You might wonder if it can possibly work, but then it turns out beautifully and with less work than you might have expected. What's different about Domini is that, although she is a professional cook, she understands what it is like to feed a family, day in, day out, including school lunches and all the rest. She doesn't assume that anyone has a store cupboard brimming with exotic and delicious things; rather, she knows that most of us operate out of a fridge with less than inspiring contents. Don't worry, she'll say, if you don't have such and such, another ingredient will do just as well – in fact, it may be even better. In this way she coaxes you to cook, to give this or that recipe a try. It's like having a friend in the kitchen with you, urging you on, telling you to relax and pouring you a glass of wine at exactly the right moment.

Orna Mulcahy
Managing Editor Features, *The Irish Times*

introduction

First of all, thank you for buying this book! Clearly you have decided that you want to do something about that gnawing question that regularly hovers as dinnertime approaches. Yes, it's the one we all face and can never seem to answer, despite the plethora of books that may sit on our shelves. 'What on earth am I going to cook for dinner?' I wouldn't mind but I am actually a cook, so I have little excuse. The other problem I face is that the countdown to dinner is one where I inevitably try to pack in far too many tasks as the day moves into the home stretch. This furious cramming to get things done often means that my lofty plans for dinner end up resembling Gulag grub, simply because time is allotted to work or general chores instead of supper. It's at this precise time that I find myself daydreaming about ways to buy myself some extra time. Ideally, this means less time spent on fiddly, multi-stage recipes and more devoted to sniffing out simple dishes that avoid messy prep and keep washing-up to a minimum. There are some dishes in the book that are more luxurious and would be considered 'treat' dinners, but the vast majority are quick, hassle-free dinners that you can get on the table within an hour.

I've been writing for *The Irish Times* since 2008, which gave me plenty of recipes to work with when choosing which dishes would go into *Dinner*. I've seen a lot of things change over the last six years, so going back over old columns was a wonderful trip down memory lane. However, what has been constant throughout is my love of great flavours, ease, comfort and, a lot of the time, healthy, nutritious recipes.

Cooking requires a bit of effort – there is no getting away from it – but sitting down at the table to eat something you have prepared from scratch is worth every ounce of the time and care you dedicated to it. I hope you find some favourites in this book so that the familiar question, 'What's for dinner?', will not be as daunting with a few of these recipes up your sleeve. If you would like to get in touch, please do at dkemp@irish-times.com. Again, thank you for buying this book. I really hope you'll enjoy cooking from it!

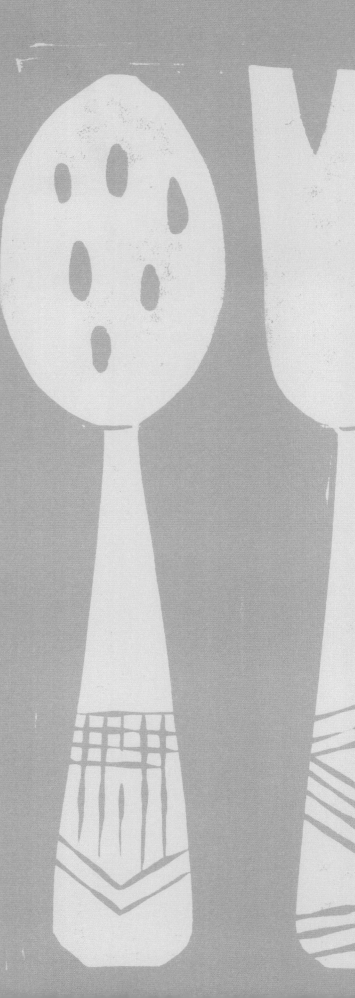

CHICKEN, TURKEY & DUCK

O1

lemon spiced chicken with chickpeas

Good glug of olive oil

1 onion, peeled and diced

4 skinless chicken breasts, diced into bite-sized chunks

Salt and pepper

$^1/_2$ cinnamon stick (approx. 8 cm)

1 tsp ground coriander

1 tsp ground cumin

Zest and juice of 2 lemons

Approx. 400 g chickpeas, drained and rinsed

350 ml chicken stock

Approx. 250 g baby spinach

This lovely chicken and chickpea dinner can be whipped up very quickly, and 'adding greens' can just mean a bag of rocket or some Swiss chard, rather than baby spinach. Iron-rich leafy greens with an astringent flavour will help to balance out the chickpeas and the warm spices. You could also do this as a vegetarian dish by removing the chicken and sautéing some mushrooms or hunks of sweet potato and using vegetable stock instead of chicken stock.

Serves 4

In a large saucepan with a lid, heat up the olive oil and sauté the onion until soft. Add in the chicken and turn up the heat and season well. When you're starting to get good colour on the chicken, add in the spices and continue to cook to get even more colour on the chicken.

After another few minutes, add the lemon juice and zest. Then add in the chickpeas and stock. Mix well, put the lid on and simmer very gently for about 12–15 minutes. Taste and adjust seasoning and then add in the spinach before serving and let it just wilt. You can add stock if you would like it to be a bit more soupy or like a stew. You can also simmer without a lid if you prefer something dryer. Don't forget to remove and discard the cinnamon stick before serving.

02

turkey burgers with quick 'cream' sauce

500 g minced turkey meat
1 courgette, grated
1 bunch spring onions, chopped
1 egg, beaten
Bunch mint, chopped
Bunch coriander, chopped
2 cloves garlic, peeled and crushed
Salt and pepper
Good pinch cayenne pepper
Olive oil

To serve:
3 tbsp Greek yoghurt
1–2 tbsp chutney or relish

These turkey burgers, based on an Ottolenghi recipe, are a real crowd-pleaser that everyone will enjoy. They are also easy to make and pretty lean, as I don't bother searing them before baking.

Serves 4–6

Preheat the oven to 200°C. Mix all the ingredients for the burgers together, season well and shape into small patties – about 7 cm across and 3 cm thick. Place in the fridge to chill down. Before cooking, drizzle them with olive oil and place them on a parchment-lined baking tray. Bake for 30 minutes until starting to brown, turning them over once, about 20 minutes in, to brown both sides.

These are lovely served with a yoghurt/relish combo – you just mix Greek yoghurt with some chutney or even courgette or tomato relish.

Recommended side: *Avocado and roast beetroot salad with blood orange (p. 262) or Rhubarb and lentil salad (p. 276).*

03

chicken with red peppers and olives

1 jar of roasted red peppers

8 pieces of chicken, skin removed

10 cloves garlic, unpeeled

Bay leaves

Bunch rosemary

110 g jar black stoned olives

100 ml olive oil

1 glass white wine

This chicken dish is just magic in flavour, and you can use either fresh or jarred peppers. Stoned black kalamata olives just seem to make everything taste good. There is also plenty of garlic in this dish, but the cloves are left whole and unpeeled. You may worry that it will be too dry, but as long as you have a heavy-duty casserole pot with a tight-fitting lid, you will find that everything cooks in its own wonderful juices, with the olives and peppers providing a rich blanket of flavour. Using chicken legs or thighs and a bit of breast ensures that the meat stays moist.

Serves 4–6

Preheat the oven to 180°C. Drain enough of the red pepper pieces to amount to two whole ones and chop them into thick strips. This is usually about 4–6 whole pieces of pepper from the jar.

Toss all the ingredients together in the pot that you will use to cook it in, or if easier, in a big bowl and then transfer to a casserole pot with a tight-fitting lid.

Bake for at least 30 minutes and then remove the lid and give it a little stir, trying to get at some of the juices at the bottom to drizzle onto the top parts, and bake for 15 more minutes. You should have fully-cooked, beautiful, moist chicken pieces. Serve with some nice bread, a platter of cheese and a big green salad.

Recommended sides: *Warm tomato salad (p. 280) or Balsamic potatoes (p. 274).*

04

roast chicken bake

Approx. 300 g cherry tomatoes

2 red onions, peeled and quartered

1 red pepper and 1 yellow pepper, de-seeded and roughly chopped (1- to 2-inch pieces)

8 skinless, boneless chicken thighs

4 cloves garlic, peeled and crushed

Few springs thyme or oregano or rosemary

1 tsp smoked paprika

2 tbsp olive oil

2 tbsp balsamic vinegar

100 ml white wine

Salt and pepper

This chicken dish has a Mediterranean feel to it and will serve as a reminder of summer when you most need it. If you get your butcher to debone the thighs as part of your order, this dish takes less than 10 minutes to prepare. It's that easy. Simply mix all the ingredients together in a bowl, transfer onto a tray, bung it in the oven and voilà! It really is the ultimate no-brainer dinner. All you need is some squishy bread to mop up all those lovely juices.

Serves 4

Preheat the oven to 180°C. Are you ready? It's so simple: put all the ingredients in a bowl, toss them together and season really well (good seasoning is essential here). Then swap the bowl for a roasting tray and bake for 45–50 minutes. This smells divine and tastes even better.

Recommended side: *Chargrilled asparagus with marinated courgette and halloumi (p. 278).*

05

chicken autumn pie

Approx. 130 g pancetta or bacon
lardons

1 good tbsp olive oil

1 leek, trimmed and sliced

1 celeriac, peeled and diced

Thyme leaves

Salt and pepper

4 skinless chicken breasts, diced

50 ml white wine

300 ml chicken stock

200 ml crème fraîche

200 g puff pastry, thawed

Flour for dusting

1 egg yolk

The original recipe for this chicken pie by Gordon Ramsay was more like chicken fricassée with a lid on it, but by using the same principles and easing up on some of the 'celebrity chef' extra steps, you get a simple and very tasty dish. It really is easy to do and makes a decent-sized dish.

Serves 4–6

Preheat the oven to 200°C. Fry the pancetta or bacon with a little oil until good and crisp and then remove from the pan. Add the rest of the oil and sauté the vegetables. Add the thyme leaves and season lightly. Mix well and then add in the chicken and again season lightly.

When you feel you are getting little hints of colour on some of the chicken or vegetables, you can add in the wine and let it bubble away and evaporate. Then slowly add in the stock and bring up to a gentle simmer. Cook for about 10 minutes and then remove the lid and cook for another 5 minutes to reduce the stock down. Add in the crème fraîche and the lardons.

At this stage, it should be cooked through, but you need to cook it a little longer and gently reduce the sauce to a nicer and thicker consistency. Taste the 'stew' and tweak the seasoning.

While this is finishing, dust your countertop with flour and roll out the pastry to fit a suitably sized gratin dish, or even to make 4–6 individual ones. Lay the pastry out on greaseproof paper and brush with egg yolk that you've 'let down' with a little salt – beating it with salt makes it a little runnier and easier to brush. Brush lightly and then bake for 10–15 minutes until puffed up and golden brown. Serve the pie in individual dishes with some pastry on top.

06

saffron chicken and rice

1 cinnamon stick

1 tsp ground coriander

1 tsp cumin seeds

Few cardamom seeds

50 g butter

500 g basmati rice

650 ml chicken stock

100 g currants

2 tbsp olive oil

8 chicken thighs

Salt and pepper

2–3 onions, peeled and very thinly sliced

6 cloves garlic, peeled and sliced

3-inch piece ginger, peeled and sliced

1 chilli, thinly sliced

Good pinch saffron

2 tbsp milk

Bag frozen peas (optional)

Handful chopped coriander (optional)

I absolutely love this dish: great flavours that can be tweaked to suit your taste.

Serves 4–6

Preheat the oven to 180°C. In a large, heavy-based saucepan that has a lid, heat up the cinnamon, coriander, cumin, cardamom and butter together until it smells delicious.

Meanwhile, rinse the rice very well in a sieve until the water runs clear, and then drain before adding in the rice to the spices and mixing well. Cook the rice in the butter and spices for about 3 minutes. Add about 500 ml stock and cook, uncovered, until the water has evaporated. Then remove from the heat and stir in the currants. Put the rice aside in a bowl, and clean out the saucepan to use for the next bit of cooking.

Heat the oil and then fry the chicken pieces, skin-side down at first. A lot of fat will come off them as the chicken skin renders down. Fry until they have really good colour and then turn over and fry on the fleshy side. Season well.

The chicken skin should become so crisp that it starts to come away from the thighs. Transfer the chicken thighs – they will still be quite raw, so you need to wash your hands carefully before and after handling them – onto a plate. Using a fork or tongs, pull away as much skin as you can and discard.

Leave the chicken on the plate and then fry the onion slices in the chicken fat in the saucepan. Cook until starting to go soft with a good dark brown colour. Take your time and don't let them burn. Add in the garlic, ginger and chilli. Mix well and season. Then transfer the onions to a plate.

This is the final bit. Put the chicken in a layer at the bottom of the pan. Pour in the 150 ml chicken stock. Then top with the onions and then the spiced rice. Finally mix the saffron with the milk and pour on top. Cover and cook out for about 45 minutes in the oven. Let it settle for about 10 minutes and then fluff up. Pick out the thighs, and to make it even less hassle to eat – if that's possible – gently pull the chicken away from the bones with a fork and then discard the bones. You can also bulk it out with some frozen peas when reheating.

07

chicken braised in red wine

50 g butter

1 chicken, cut into 8 pieces

Salt and pepper

1 large white onion, peeled and diced

100 g smoked bacon, diced

16 button mushrooms, cut in half

2 cloves garlic, peeled and crushed

1 tbsp flour

3 tbsp tomato purée

250 ml red wine

500 ml chicken or vegetable stock

1 tbsp sugar

This is a very simple chicken braised in red wine, or 'coq au vin' if you prefer. It is decidedly uncheffy and makes a very tasty stew that sits on the stove, rather than in the oven. It takes one whole chicken, which your butcher should cut up into eight pieces for you. It serves four people very comfortably with nice leftovers. Remember, if you don't have stock or a stock cube, use less water, a bit more wine and more salt.

Serves 4

Use a hefty saucepan with a lid. Add half the butter and then fry the chicken in batches. Season really well, and when well browned, drain on a plate with kitchen paper. Finish off the chicken, removing it to the plate as you go.

Put in the rest of the butter and fry the onions until just starting to caramelise. Then throw in the bacon, fry until the onions get some more colour and then add the mushrooms and garlic. Mix well until it's tasty and brown and check the seasoning. Add the flour and cook out, mixing with the fat in the pan, for at least 1 minute. It will absorb a lot of the fat and may tease you into thinking it's all going to burn. Turn down the heat if you need to, but make sure you cook out the flour or the taste of raw flour will haunt the final dish.

Next add the tomato purée to the onion/mushroom/bacon mix, and then add the wine, stock and sugar. Stir, bring up to the boil and taste before you add the chicken. If you think you need to skim any fat, do so by taking it off the heat and skimming with a metal spoon – but it should be fine.

When you are happy with the sauce, carefully add the chicken back in, bed it down, put the lid on (and maybe remove the lid partially, half-way through) and simmer gently for about 50 minutes. If it's bubbling away furiously, then all the water will evaporate and it will burn. It needs to end up the right consistency, so play around with your lid and monitor the thickness of the sauce. You can always add a glass of water if it's gone too thick or starting to burn. If it's watery and insipid, turn up the heat to reduce the sauce to concentrate the flavour. If you have time, let it sit on the stove off the heat for about 30 minutes or so and then reheat before serving. It always tastes better after it's had a little breather.

chicken with walnut sauce

200 g walnuts

1 onion, peeled and diced

Olive oil

4 tsp smoked sweet paprika

3 cloves garlic, peeled and crushed

$^{1}/_{2}$ tsp cayenne pepper

100 g breadcrumbs

Juice of 4 lemons

Big bunch parsley

3 tbsp plain or Greek yoghurt

6 chicken breasts, skinless, chopped into chunks

Salt and pepper

750 ml chicken stock

It's no oil painting, but this Circassian chicken – a traditional Turkish recipe – is tasty, nutty and unusual. It would work very well as a party dish as part of a larger affair as it tastes great at room temperature. Serve with plenty of vegetables or with some salads and nice bread to mop up all the delicious blobs of sauce that will be left on your plate.

Serves 4–6

Toast the walnuts on a baking tray for about 10 minutes at 160°C until lightly toasted. Sweat the onion in plenty of olive oil until soft and then add in the paprika, garlic and cayenne pepper. Season well. Add in the breadcrumbs and a bit more olive oil. Then take off the heat and cool slightly while you transfer the walnuts into a food processor. Add in the onion and breadcrumb mixture and some lemon juice and parsley and a bit of yoghurt. Process, adding in the rest of the lemon juice and yoghurt to taste. Adjust seasoning and set aside.

Heat up more olive oil (I do this in the same pan I cook the onion in) and fry the chicken over a high heat to get some colour on it. Season well and turn the chunks over. When you have good colour, gradually add the stock so that you are deglazing the pan and also poaching the chicken. Cook gently, adding in the rest of the chicken until most of the stock has evaporated and the chicken is fully cooked. Allow to cool slightly and add the chicken to the walnut sauce. Mix well.

The walnut sauce should be thick enough to coat the chicken well, but not so thick that you feel like you are eating poached chicken smothered in peanut butter – or walnut butter. The sauce should be loose enough to be pleasant in the mouth. It then becomes unbelievably moreish.

Recommended sides: *Quinoa and tomato panzanella-style salad (p. 296) or Wild rice and sweetcorn salad (p. 294).*

09

chicken with sherry and mushrooms

60 g packs dried mushrooms

Good knob butter

Olive oil

4–6 chicken breasts, cut into chunks

Salt and pepper

2 onions, peeled and very finely chopped

150 g chestnut mushrooms, roughly chopped

2 cloves garlic, peeled and crushed

Few sprigs thyme

150 ml Marsala or port or sherry

300 ml chicken stock

100 ml crème fraîche

Small bunch parsley, chopped

This is one of those dishes for which you can use any fortified wine, including port or Marsala, but good sherry always works well in cooking. The flavours are admittedly pretty grown up and it does contain alcohol, so it's unlikely children will be partaking. The alcohol content is worth bearing in mind, as even with plenty of simmering, a little alcohol content will always remain.

Serves 4

Preheat the oven to 180°C. Soak the dried mushrooms in a small amount of boiling water for up to an hour. In a large saucepan, heat up some butter and olive oil and then sear the chicken in batches until good and brown. Season really well and once it colours, transfer to a bowl and set aside for a few minutes.

Try to leave some fat in the pan and sauté the onions in it until soft. Then add in the chestnut mushrooms. Strain the dried mushrooms, saving the water. Strain the water again to remove any grit. Roughly chop the dried mushrooms and put into the saucepan. Season well and then when soft, add the garlic and thyme. Then turn up the heat and add in the sherry.

Cook over a high heat and then add in the chicken pieces and any juice. Add the stock, strained mushroom water and then the crème fraîche. Mix really well and then cover with a lid and put in the oven for about 30 minutes.

Allow to settle for a minute and then taste. It should be rich and delicious. Adjust seasoning if necessary or reduce the sauce by removing the chicken and cooking the sauce on the stove for a few minutes. Then scatter with some parsley. Serve with mash, wild rice or just some good bread and green salad.

Recommended side: *Leek and bread pudding (p. 298).*

10

stuffed chicken with mozzarella and herbs

2 cloves garlic, peeled and crushed

4–8 anchovy fillets

1–2 tsp capers

200 g mozzarella, diced (approx. 2 balls)

4 skinless chicken breasts

80 g breadcrumbs

Few sprigs thyme, finely chopped

Small bunch parsley, finely chopped

40 g Parmesan, finely grated

1 egg, beaten

4 tbsp olive oil

Big knob butter

The real joy of mozzarella is in the texture, but it is really tasty in this gutsy chicken dish. It will be very popular with the family, but don't be put off by the anchovies, even if you aren't a fan. The brown tinned ones are little slithers of flavour and are not as strong as the silver pickled ones you get in some delis, but you might be better off not mentioning the anchovies regardless, in case they put people off. You can tell them afterwards, as they gaze adoringly at you, marvelling at your domestic skills.

Serves 4

Preheat the oven to 180°C. Then sort out the stuffing: mix the garlic, anchovies, capers and mozzarella in a bowl. Mush it and squish it with spoon or fork until you have a rustic-looking mixture.

Next get a gratin dish that will fit all four chicken breasts. Slit each breast horizontally, put it in the dish and then fill each slit with a quarter of the stuffing. You can secure them closed with toothpicks and then put into the fridge to chill down until ready to cook.

When you are ready to cook, mix the breadcrumbs, thyme, parsley and Parmesan together and season well. Then take each chicken breast, dip in the egg, then pat or dip into the breadcrumbs and put back in the gratin dish. Drizzle the oil on top of the chicken, dot with butter and bake for at least 40 minutes until golden brown. If you have chilled the chicken down well enough, the topping will go all crunchy and the chicken won't be overcooked.

Recommended side: *Summer crunchy caprese (p. 290).*

11

poached chicken, green bean and peach salad

1 whole chicken

2 bay leaves

3-inch piece ginger, peeled

1 onion, peeled and quartered

Salt

zest and juice of 1 orange

zest and juice of 1 lemon

4 ripe peaches, stoned and cut into quarters

2 tbsp honey

Salt and pepper

Approx. 500 g green beans

Handful cashew nuts, toasted

100 ml olive oil

3 tbsp wholegrain mustard

1 clove garlic, peeled and crushed

Bunch parsley or basil, chopped

This green bean and peach salad uses a poaching method with which to cook the chicken, but if you had enough meat left over from roasting a chicken, you could use that. You could also use the leftover poaching liquid for making soup but it would be good to skim it occasionally and really reduce it down before using it.

Serves 6

Put the chicken in a large stockpot with a lid. Cover with water and add the bay leaves, ginger, onion, salt and the lemon and orange zest. Bring up to a simmer and cook gently for about 40 minutes and then turn off the heat. Add the orange juice and let it sit in the water until cool enough to handle and tear up (about an hour).

You could get the rest of the ingredients ready in the interim so you just have to toss everything together at the last minute. Put the peaches in a roasting tray, drizzle with honey and season generously. Grill for a few minutes until they start to char. Pour a little olive oil on them and leave them until ready to serve.

Blanch the green beans in boiling water for a minute and then refresh in cold water to stop the cooking process. Drain and set aside.

Stick the cashew nuts in the oven to toast. Whisk together the olive oil with the mustard, garlic and lemon juice. Season well and pour in the juices from the grilled peaches to sweeten. Then shred the meat from the chicken (which should still be warm) discarding the skin and arranging the meat on a nice platter. Toss the green beans in a little of the dressing and arrange on top and scatter with the grilled peaches and nuts. Add some herbs and a little more dressing and serve so that everyone can help themselves.

12

grilled saffron and chilli chicken

Pinch saffron

1 large bunch mint

2 chillies, deseeded and roughly chopped

3 cloves garlic, peeled and crushed

Zest and juice of 2 limes

Good pinch dried mint

2-inch piece ginger, peeled and diced

1 tsp ground cardamom

Tiny squeeze honey

Salt and black pepper

8 boneless, skinless chicken thighs

Few glugs olive oil

Cardamom, ginger and saffron are aromatics that lend great flavour to anything. However, while ginger and cardamom are modest enough in price, saffron is one of the most expensive ingredients around, yet it is a great flavour and well worth trying if you can. Along with goat's cheese, beetroot and coriander, it's a flavour you begin to like more as an adult. It's kind of leathery and musky, which are odd flavours to want. However, it holds up when combined with spices and creates a really well-rounded flavour, exactly as it does in this chicken dish, which works a treat as casual, fun, party food.

Serves 4

Soak the saffron threads in a mean tablespoon of boiling water in a cup and leave to sit while you get the marinade ready. Remove the really stalky bits from the mint and then put it into your food processor along with the chillies, garlic, lime juice and zest, mint, ginger, cardamom, honey and seasoning. Give it a blast and add in the saffron threads and water. If it won't whizz, add a little olive oil and then blitz until you have a loose salsa that's reasonably fine in texture.

Put the chicken thighs in a shallow dish and pour over the marinade and try to leave for at least an hour to marinate. It really doesn't need to be done overnight. To cook, heat up your chargrill pan until smoking and cook 4 at a time (unless you have a very big and hot chargrill pan). They take a little while, so don't overload the pan.

If you have a very large batch to do (say if you are doubling the recipe) then sear them all really well on the chargrill until they are very well coloured on both sides and then put them in a large roasting tin and finish cooking them in the oven – for 30 minutes at 180°C.

They will also cook easily on the BBQ, but do remember that thighs are often a bit thicker than chicken breasts, so can take a little longer. If you can baste them or pour over any excess marinade while they are cooking in the oven, do so.

Recommended side: *Carrot salad with ginger and lemon (p. 254).*

13

roast chicken with fennel, marmalade and mustard

10–12 pieces of chicken (thighs and legs are good)

100 ml white wine

4 tbsp olive oil

Juice of 1 lemon

2 tbsp wholegrain mustard

3 fennel bulbs cut into half-inch slices

1 red onion, peeled and sliced

1 head garlic, left whole

1 orange, sliced into rounds and then cut into half-moons

1 tbsp thyme leaves

2 tbsp fennel seeds

2 tsp coriander seeds

2 tbsp marmalade

Salt and pepper

Flat-leaf parsley, chopped

Chicken is always a good choice for big groups, as it is really the ultimate crowd-pleaser. It also doesn't have to be bland, which is a myth that some have built up around chicken. This recipe is simplicity itself – more assembly than alchemy. The classic combination of citrus (yes, that's marmalade in there) and warm, aniseedy fennel is very tasty. The mustard might seem like it won't work, but in fact it gives it additional depth and warmth.

Serves 4–6

Preheat the oven to 170°C. Place the whole lot in a large bowl and mix well so that everything gets coated in everything. Refrigerate until ready to cook. You can easily bulk this out, making a bigger batch with whatever ingredients you have most of – it doesn't need to be in perfect proportion – so it's great for when there are a few extra mouths to feed.

When ready to cook, split between a couple of gratin dishes so that you have one layer of ingredients rather than loading it all into one pan. Season well and bake for 45–50 minutes, loosely covered with foil, which you can remove for the last ten minutes to add some colour and caramelisation. Serve garnished with chopped parsley.

Recommended side: *White bean and mushroom gratin (p. 256).*

14

shredded duck salad

6 legs duck confit (available in most good delis or butchers)

1 head Chinese cabbage, finely shredded

1 bunch spring onions, finely chopped

1 small green chilli, de-seeded and finely sliced

1 ripe mango, peeled and sliced

Bunch coriander, chopped

1 tsp sesame seeds

Seeds from 2 pomegranates

1 tsp sumac

For the dressing:

1 tbsp sesame oil

50 ml olive oil

2 tbsp soy sauce (use tamari if cooking for coeliacs)

1 tbsp horseradish sauce

1 tbsp runny honey

1 small cloves garlic, peeled and crushed

1-inch piece ginger, peeled and grated

Ready-prepared duck confit is a great standby. By warming it up and shredding the meat you have instant deliciousness to add to any array of leaves.

Serves 6

Prepare the duck confit as per the instructions; this usually involves placing the trays in a low oven until the fat has melted and the legs can be removed easily. If you like, keep some of the fat for roast potatoes.

Gently remove the skin from the duck, then place the skin on baking parchment on a tray, sprinkle each piece lightly with a pinch of sumac and cook in a hot oven (200°C) until crisp – think of it as the classy version of pork scratchings. Crunch up and put aside to sprinkle on the salad just before serving.

Meanwhile, flake the meat carefully off the leg and thigh bones. Whisk all the dressing ingredients together, or shake them in a jar. On a large, flat plate or shallow bowl, toss the duck with the lettuce and dressing. You may want to add some of the pomegranate juice to loosen up the dressing. Arrange and scatter the rest of the ingredients on the platter and let everyone dig in.

15

salt and peppa chook

4 star anise
3 tsp Szechuan peppercorns
1 tsp fennel seeds
1 cinnamon stick
6 cloves
Few tbsp olive oil
Zest of 2 limes
1 good tsp sea salt
Black pepper
Few sprigs thyme
6–8 pieces of chicken

This is a very easy and tasty recipe. It uses one whole chicken cut into 6–8 pieces, which easily feeds 5 people. You could ask your butcher to chop it up for you or else just buy a selection of legs, thighs and breasts. If you want to do it for 8–10, then double the spices and just get as many chicken pieces as you need.

Serves 5

Put all the spices in a small saucepan and gently heat for a minute to dry-roast them. Grind them either in your grinder, or a pestle and mortar, or pour into a cup and crush them with the end of a rolling pin. Pour the crushed, dry-roasted spices back into the saucepan – no need to heat up – and add the olive oil. Add the rest of the ingredients (except the chicken) and mix well. The residual heat from the saucepan will gently warm through the olive oil and other ingredients, which will make it easier to pour and rub onto the chicken.

Put the chicken in a roasting tray and pour on the oily spice mixture. Rub the meat well, wash your hands well and marinate the chicken for an hour or overnight if possible, covering the chicken with cling film and keeping it in the fridge.

When you're ready to cook, you can either bake this in the oven at 190°C for about 25–30 minutes (less if you're just using breast meat) or cook for 15 minutes in the oven and finish off on a barbecue. Either way it tastes great.

red pepper and chilli sauce

3 red chillies, deseeded
4 cloves garlic, peeled
4 red peppers, deseeded
3-inch piece ginger, peeled
1 tsp salt
100 ml rice wine vinegar
100 ml water
100 g sugar

Put the chillies, garlic, red peppers and ginger in a food processor or blender, along with the salt, vinegar and water and blitz till pulp-like. Pour into a saucepan and heat gently adding the sugar. Simmer for 20–30 minutes until the sauce has reduced by a third. Check the seasoning, allow to cool down and serve. It should last in the fridge for a week.

Recommended side: Broccoli salad with avocado and chilli dressing (p. 266).

16

yoghurt chicken

1 tsp coriander seeds, lightly crushed

200 g Greek yoghurt

1 tsp salt

Pepper

Juice of 2 limes or lemons

1 big bunch coriander (approx. 25 g)

4 skinless chicken breasts, cut into strips

Olive oil

This dish used to be called 'Coriander chicken', because the recipe is all about the coriander, but my kids baulk at fresh coriander, so I leave it out. I'm just happy they don't really notice the coriander seeds. If you haven't acquired any sort of fondness for coriander, feel free to substitute some flat-leaf parsley, mint or basil.

Serves 4

Crush the coriander seeds in a pestle and mortar, or put them in a cup and squish them with the end of a rolling pin. Mix the yoghurt with the salt, pepper, lime juice and coriander seeds. Roughly chop the coriander and mix in with the yoghurt. Add the chicken and mix well. If you can marinate this for anything from 1 hour to overnight, it'll be much better.

Turn your grill up high and spread the chicken onto a baking tray or roasting tin. Drizzle with some olive oil and grill, turning the chicken occasionally as the yoghurt chars quite easily. When it is cooked through, serve hot or warm. It is also delicious served cold in sandwiches the next day.

Recommended side: *Chickpea and coriander salad (p. 250).*

cola chicken

8 boneless chicken thighs

330 ml cola

60 ml soy sauce

2 tbsp five-spice powder

1 tsp cumin seeds

1 tsp coriander seeds

1 onion, peeled and finely chopped

4 cloves garlic, peeled and chopped

Salt and pepper

This dish is inspired by the South American restaurant cookbook, Ceviche. It's a bit of fun and a twist on the usual cola and ham dish you see at Christmastime. It is extremely tasty, and the meat in chicken thighs is so much better than that on the breast. You may have to ask your butcher to prep the thighs for you, but they are well worth it. This is a very moreish dish.

Serves 4

Preheat the oven to 200°C. Put the chicken into a gratin dish. (I recommend lining the gratin dish with parchment paper. It means things don't get as sticky as possible, but it does save on the washing-up – it's up to you.) Mix all the other ingredients together and pour over the chicken. Bake for about 30–40 minutes. The chicken should be nice and crispy and the sauce reduced a little. If you feel it's drying up too much, cover with tinfoil or add a couple of tablespoons of water during cooking.

Some readers have said that it took ages for the liquid to get sticky, even after 40 minutes. If that happens, pour off the excess liquid and simmer in a small saucepan until it's getting thick. Then pour it back onto the chicken and things should look tasty after another 10 minutes in the oven.

Recommended side: *Baked potatoes with crisp kale, bacon and crème fraîche with verjus (p. 272).*

butter chicken

4 skinless chicken breasts, diced

1 tbsp olive or coconut oil

75 g butter

2 onions, diced

Bunch of coriander, chopped

For the marinade:

3-inch piece ginger, peeled and diced

6 cloves garlic, peeled and sliced

1 red chilli, de-seeded and chopped

3 whole cloves

4 cardamom pods

150 ml Greek yoghurt

50 g ground almonds

1 tsp garam masala

$1/2$ tsp turmeric

$1/4$ tsp ground cinnamon

A dish called 'butter chicken' may not sound very appealing or particularly healthy, but this recipe is not that bad for you, as most other versions are laden with cream. It also tastes delicious. It would be lovely with some wholegrain basmati rice or black sticky rice.

Serves 4

To make the marinade, put all the ingredients into a food processor and blitz, adding a little water to loosen it if it's too thick. Season well. Put the marinade into a bowl and add the chicken. Marinate overnight if possible, or at least from morning till evening.

When you're ready to cook, heat up the olive or coconut oil and butter, sweat the chopped onions over a gentle heat for 10 minutes with the lid on until very soft. Add the chicken with the marinade and cook gently for 30 minutes until cooked. If the sauce is still a little thick, add some water, but it loosens up as it cooks and becomes a little more watery.

Cook with the lid on and taste after 30 minutes. Season and take off the lid if you want to thicken up the sauce. Serve with basmati rice and some coriander.

rye and mustard chicken with red cabbage

For the chicken goujons:
2–3 slices rye bread, stale
1 tbsp caraway seeds
Salt and pepper
4 skinless chicken breasts
50 g flour
2 eggs, beaten
Sunflower oil

For the cabbage:
1 knob butter
1 small red cabbage, finely sliced
1 tbsp honey
100 ml red wine vinegar
100 ml cider vinegar
Salt and pepper

For the sauce:
4 tbsp Dijon mustard
2 tbsp crème fraîche
1 tbsp dill, finely chopped

This chicken and red cabbage main course is a bit different and surprisingly easy to prepare. The cabbage can be done beforehand and heated up, and the chicken goujons breaded and ready to go in the oven, no frying involved. Bliss.

Serves 4

Preheat the oven to 150°C. Grind the bread into crumbs in a blender and bake in the oven for about 20 minutes until 'dry'. Mix the caraway seeds into the crumbs and season well. Turn the oven up to 180°C.

Next, cut the chicken into goujons/fingers. Dip the chicken into flour, then the beaten egg and finally the breadcrumbs until well coated, and place on an oiled baking tray. Drizzle with a bit more oil and bake for 30 minutes until crisp.

To make the cabbage, heat the butter in a saucepan and when melted, add the cabbage and soften for a few minutes over a low heat. Then add the vinegars, honey and salt and pepper. Cook until soft but not melting – about 25 minutes.

Finally, for the sauce, just mix the mustard, crème fraîche and dill together.

To serve, perch some chicken on top of a bed of cabbage, with the sauce on the side.

20

coq au vin

Like the chicken braised in red wine, this is another version of a classic coq au vin. This dish does really taste of the vin part, but feel free to use half a bottle and reduce the liquid for less time at the end. If you don't add in the flour, you may have to reduce the cooking sauce down a bit at the end.

Serves 6

2 tbsp olive oil
50 g butter
8–10 chicken pieces: breasts, thighs, legs, with skin on
Salt and pepper
10 pieces smoked streaky bacon, diced
1–2 onions, peeled and finely diced
250 g button mushrooms, cut into quarters
6 cloves garlic, peeled and sliced
2 bay leaves
Few sprigs thyme
2 tbsp tomato purée
1 tbsp flour
500 ml chicken stock
1 bottle red wine

Preheat the oven to 160°C. Heat some olive oil and a little butter in a large saucepan with a lid that's also ovenproof. When good and hot, fry the chicken pieces (in batches if necessary), until brown on all sides and season the chicken really well. Put the chicken pieces to one side, and then drain out the fat from the pan and discard.

Heat the rest of the olive oil and butter and fry the diced bacon until golden brown and then add the onions and sweat until soft. Then add the mushrooms, garlic, bay leaves, thyme and tomato purée. Mix really well and season. Then add in the flour and stir well and cook for a few minutes. Then add in the stock and wine gradually, stirring so that not too many lumps form.

When the mixture is simmering, add the chicken back in carefully. Put in the oven and cook for about an hour. You may want to remove the lid halfway through cooking if you want to make the sauce thicker, or for coeliacs, who won't have added the flour.

Alternatively, remove the chicken and then put the saucepan back on the hob and boil gently until reduced sufficiently. This dish can also be cooled down fully and reheated until simmering for at least 5 minutes. Serve with mashed potato or rice.

chicken, apple and flageolet bean casserole

250 g flageolet beans
Olive oil
8 chicken pieces
4 sausages (optional)
2 onions, peeled and sliced
2–3 dessert apples, peeled and chopped into chunks
1 tbsp plain flour
Few sprigs rosemary
Few bay leaves
500 ml stock
50 ml crème fraîche
Splash tarragon vinegar
Bunch tarragon, chopped

I'm a big fan of using tinned beans at home, especially tins of chickpeas, kidney beans and cannellini beans, but this is one of those recipes that wouldn't work half as well with tinned beans. So if you can, do a bit of bean-soaking the morning before and give them a blast of boiling the night before, so they are ready to go for baking the next evening. It sounds a bit more hassle than it is, but getting into the habit of soaking beans means you're thinking ahead when it comes to planning dinner, which can't be a bad thing.

Serves 4

Soak the beans for 8–10 hours in lots of salted water. Drain the beans, rinse well and simmer in plenty of water until nearly tender for 30–40 minutes.

Preheat the oven to 190°C. Heat the olive oil in a heavy-based saucepan, then season and brown the chicken well in batches and set aside. Fry the sausages until brown, remove and set aside.

Next heat the onions in the same pan as the fat. When the onion is soft, add the apples. When they're soft but not coloured, sprinkle the flour on top and stir so that the flour absorbs the excess fat and cooks out. Add the rosemary and bay leaves. Then add the stock gradually, but keep stirring constantly. Add the chicken, the sausage and the cooked beans back into the saucepan.

Cook in the oven for about 40 minutes with a lid on. Check to see if you need to add more liquid halfway through the cooking time. When the chicken is cooked, add the crème fraîche, tarragon vinegar and some chopped tarragon. Check the seasoning and adjust. Serve with some bread and a nice glass of white wine.

BEEF, VEAL & VENISON

22

tagliata of beef

600–800 g fillet of beef
Salt and pepper
4 good handfuls rocket
8 portobello mushrooms,
peeled and cut into thick slices

Parmesan shavings

For the marinade:
100 ml balsamic vinegar
Good few sprigs rosemary
6 cloves garlic, peeled
200 ml olive oil

It is hard to imagine a tastier, juicer and more delicious meal with a glass of red wine than a tagliata of beef. Tagliata means 'cut', so this is a sort of sliced beef dish that can be loaded up in plenty of different ways. Restaurant versions seem to feature plenty of rocket and Parmesan shavings, but with none of the herby concoctions some chefs like. This is a sort of hybrid version, achieved by marinating the beef in a rich, thick balsamic marinade pumped full of rosemary. You can also fry chunky slices of portobello mushroom in the same marinade to serve along with the beef, which bulks out this dish nicely.

This recipe uses fillet of beef, but feel free to substitute sirloin or rib-eye if making for larger numbers, as the fillet would get very pricey.

Serves 4–6

Start by making the marinade. First remove all the leaves from the rosemary and throw away the stalks – you want a good tablespoon or two of rosemary leaves. In a blender, whizz all the ingredients together. Season the marinade, which should be dark and thick. Then pour on top of the beef and leave for a while to marinate in the fridge; a few hours would be great, overnight even better.

When ready to cook, dish up the rocket onto each plate along with some Parmesan shavings. Heat up a frying pan or chargrill until really hot. If your pan is a regular size, do this in two batches. Let the excess marinade run off the beef and then sear and brown at a very high temperature. Turn the steaks over when they no longer stick to the pan. When you have great colour on them, set aside to rest. Finish cooking any remaining steaks if necessary; otherwise fry the chunky mushrooms and pour any remaining marinade on top – they don't need much cooking. They will absorb the marinade and heat up thoroughly till they get slightly charred and burnt at the edges and are piping hot. At this stage, you can slice the beef and arrange beef slices and mushrooms on top of the rocket and serve straightaway.

23

Asian beef salad

400 g sirloin of beef, brought up to room temperature

2 tsp wasabi paste

2 tsp miso paste

Few splashes soy sauce

200 g oyster mushrooms

1 bunch spring onions, chopped

2-inch piece ginger, peeled and grated

1 clove garlic, peeled and crushed

Few leaves basil, torn

400 g mangetout

25 g sesame seeds

Olive oil

Water

You can use any lean piece of beef that's suitable for frying. This dish uses Japanese wasabi horseradish and has a real spicy Asian tang to it, which is enhanced by the soy, miso and sesame seeds. An umami taste sensation!

Serves 6–8

Take your steaks out of the fridge about an hour before you want to cook them, so they come up to room temperature. Heat a frying pan till hot. Lightly oil the steaks and when the pan is smoking, sear the sirloin on one side, brushing generously with the wasabi and miso. I do this with the back of a spoon and smear rather than brush it on. Turn it over to cook on its other side, adding a few splashes of soy or tamari to help colour the steak. Add some sesame seeds – they will hop around the place, so beware – and cook for about 2 minutes, always turning to get colour on both sides. Then remove the steak from the pan and set aside (you want it pink in the middle, and it will continue to cook off the pan).

Add a little more oil to the pan and sauté the mushrooms first in order to help sop up those juices. If the pan has become too dry or the mushrooms aren't producing enough liquid to deglaze the pan, add a few splashes of water to stop it burning. When things start to sizzle again, add the spring onions, ginger, garlic, basil and mangetout. Cook on a high heat for about three minutes. To serve, slice the beef finely, place the vegetables on a platter and scatter the beef and more sesame seeds over the top.

24

Indian mince

This mince recipe is adapted from a Diana Henry one, which she adapted from Madhur Jaffrey, so it's definitely done the rounds. It is delicious and the lime is infectiously good with it. In fact, if you reheat this dish, be sure to squeeze more lime on to it. The piquancy and sharpness of the lime just lifts the mince out of monotony.

This could be served with a big bowl of rice or else on top of naan bread. The store cupboard ingredients for this dish often lift a meal from being an ordinary 'spag bol' or shepherd's pie into something a little more lively. A few limes and some chopped coriander also do their job brilliantly.

Serves 4–6

Heat the olive oil and in batches, fry the mince on a good heat, get some colour on it and set it aside while you fry off the rest. Once you've done that, wipe the excess fat out of the pan and then sauté the onions until soft. Add the garlic, ginger and chilli, as well as the spices, and sauté on a high heat until the spices come to life and smell great. Add the beef back in and season lightly.

Then add the tomato purée and brown sugar. Mix well and add in the stock. Simmer gently for about 30 minutes with the lid off. Then taste a little, adjust the seasoning and add the frozen peas and lime juice. The peas just take a minute or two to thaw out. Taste again and serve with wedges of lime and chopped coriander.

Recommended side: *Pomegranate and green bean salad (p. 270).*

---

2 tbsp olive oil

Approx. 800 g minced beef

2 onions, peeled and very finely chopped

6 cloves garlic, peeled and finely sliced

3-inch piece ginger, peeled and sliced

1 green chilli, deseeded and sliced

1 tsp ground coriander

Pinch cumin seeds

¼ tsp cayenne pepper

1 tsp garam masala

1 tbsp tomato purée

Good pinch brown sugar

375 ml beef stock

Salt and pepper

200 g frozen peas

Bunch coriander

Juice of 2 limes

stuffed aubergines

4 aubergines

Approx. 150 ml olive oil

Salt and pepper

1 onion, peeled and diced

4 cloves garlic, peeled and chopped

600 g minced beef

Approx. 750 ml passata or 800 g chopped tomatoes

2 tsp caster sugar

Few splashes Worcestershire sauce

Approx. 170 g feta

80 g Parmesan

Chopped parsley

This recipe for stuffed aubergines was once humorously described to me as 'posh, student cuisine with a bit of Greek thrown in'. It is an apt description, as it's not too difficult to make, but it's also a very tasty and moreish dish. They go well with a fresh green salad and some crusty bread.

Serves 4–6

Preheat the oven to 180°C. Cut the aubergines in half lengthways and score the flesh as though you were marking out a diagonal tic-tac-toe board, without cutting all the way through. Brush the aubergines very generously with half the olive oil, season very well and bake for about 30 minutes until the flesh is soft and mushy and starting to colour. Allow them to cool while you get the sauce underway.

Heat the other half of the olive oil, sweat the onion and garlic until soft and just starting to brown. Add the minced meat and break it up with a wooden spoon and when fairly well cooked, add the passata or tomatoes. Turn up the heat and add the sugar and Worcestershire sauce. When it's starting to bubble and simmer, turn down the heat and cook gently for 10–15 minutes before tasting to check the seasoning.

If you are happy with the flavour, roughly chop the feta and add to the mince. Scoop out the aubergine flesh and roughly chop and add to the mince. Check the seasoning again and put the aubergines in a shallow gratin dish and spoon the mince mix on top. Sprinkle some Parmesan on top and bake for about 30–40 minutes until the cheese has melted and the aubergines are piping hot. Serve with some parsley sprinkled on top, a nice salad and some fresh bread.

26

beef rendang

1 tbsp coriander seeds

1 tsp cumin seeds

1 cinnamon stick

4 cloves

Good pinch dried chilli

1 tsp turmeric

Few glugs olive oil

2 onions, peeled and chopped

3-inch piece ginger, peeled and sliced

6 cloves garlic, peeled and sliced

2 sticks lemongrass, finely chopped

2 kg chuck/rump steak

Salt and pepper

1 tbsp soft brown sugar

800 ml coconut milk

Bunch coriander, chopped

This variation on the traditional Indonesian/Malaysian coconut-based dish may sound exotic and spicy, but it actually has very easy-going flavours. Everyone in the family, from kids to grannies, should enjoy it. It works best with plain rice but try wild rice for a change.

Serves 6–8

Put all the spices in a large saucepan and gently heat for a minute to dry-roast them. Either grind them up or pour into a cup and crush them with the end of a rolling pin. Pour the crushed, dry-roasted spices back into the saucepan and add the olive oil. Add the onion, ginger, garlic and lemongrass and sweat for a few minutes.

Add in the meat, mix so it is well coated in the spices and season well with salt and pepper and then put in the sugar. You can turn the heat up and if the meat browns a little, great. However, don't caramelise the meat at the expense of burning the spices! Now add the coconut milk. Cook for at least 2 hours on a very gentle heat.

Leave it uncovered so that it reduces, and do give it an occasional stir as it can burn the bottom of the pan. Eventually the meat should be incredibly tender, and the sauce nice and thick. Adjust the seasoning and serve on some boiled rice with loads of chopped coriander.

This is also one of those dishes that will taste very good the day after! If it has dried out too much, just add a few splashes of water, check the seasoning and it should be fine.

27

marinated skirt steak

Handful rosemary leaves, very
finely chopped

1 head garlic, peeled and
crushed

1 tin anchovies

1 tbsp Dijon mustard

1 tsp English mustard powder

Lots of black pepper

1 tsp Demerara sugar

¹/₂ bottle red wine

1 kg skirt steak, cut into 2 pieces

Skirt steak is ideal for this recipe as it is very tasty. However, it can also be quite tough if your butcher doesn't hang meat for long enough. If you wanted to spend a bit more and if you were catering for about 10 people, get a whole fillet and cook it in one long piece. Then allow it to rest and slice it thinly for your guests. It would be more expensive, but this marinade is so gutsy that it would be delicious with the bland but beautifully tender fillet. This recipe has been adapted from a Valentine Warner recipe.

Serves 4

Chuck the rosemary, garlic and anchovies (including the oil) into a saucepan and heat gently while you squish the anchovies with the back of a wooden spoon. Turn up the heat and sweat them gently. Add the mustards, pepper and sugar. Mix well and then pour in the wine and bring to the boil. Simmer gently until the mixture reduces by half. It should look a bit like purple hoisin sauce. Allow the marinade to cool fully and then roll and rub the beef with the marinade and leave for a few hours in the fridge. Turn the meat occasionally while it's marinating. Then cook the meat for about 5–7 minutes on each side on a barbecue or chargrill. Allow it to rest for at least 5–10 minutes and then carve at an angle, against the grain, into thin slices.

Recommended side: *Balsamic potatoes (p. 274) or Asparagus with miso butter (p. 246).*

28

braised beef with red wine and penne

500 g chuck steak, diced

1 bottle Chianti wine

Olive oil

Salt and pepper

1 head celery

1 red onion, peeled and diced

3 cloves garlic, peeled and diced

Small bunch sage

2 sprigs rosemary

5 juniper berries

4 cloves

30 g dried porcini mushrooms, soaked in 500 ml hot water

4 bay leaves

20 g pine nuts

500 g penne

Zest of 1 lemon

100 g Parmesan

This recipe requires a 24-hour head start, but the result is a rich, unctuous dish that you will marvel at. It can be used as a special Sunday evening dinner, and then you can flesh out the cooled leftovers with some frozen peas and freeze it so you have a tasty dish ready to go. Adapted from the brilliant River Café Cook Book.

Serves 6

Marinate the beef in the red wine overnight. Then drain the meat and keep the wine. Pat the meat dry and then heat up the olive oil in a heavy-based saucepan. When it's good and hot, add the beef and sear it all over, keeping the heat up high and seasoning the meat very well. If you find the meat is stewing rather than colouring, remove it with a slotted spoon, let any liquid evaporate, add some more olive oil and get it to the point of smoking. You really need to get some colour going.

While this is happening, roughly chop the celery, onion and garlic and chuck into the saucepan and mix well. Add the herbs and spices. Then add in the mushrooms – which you can drain and roughly chop – and add in ³/₄ of the reserved wine that you marinated the beef in and most of the mushroom soaking water. (It's probably good to strain this water a bit as it can sometimes be a bit gritty.) Bring the meat up to a simmer, add the bay leaves, cover and gently simmer for at least 3–4 hours over a very low heat. Top up with any remaining water or wine to keep the sauce 'wet'.

It's best to let the meat cool down, settle and then 'mash' with a fork. Then add enough olive oil to give it a saucy unctuousness and reheat gently. Boil up the pasta, drain and toss with the beef sauce and pine nuts (which you can lightly toast in a dry pan) add in some lemon zest and adjust the seasoning. Top with Parmesan and serve.

29

meatloaf and crushed tomato sauce

Olive oil

500 g minced beef

500 g minced pork

100 g breadcrumbs

3 cloves garlic, peeled and chopped

150 g Parmesan, grated

1 tbsp sundried tomato paste

Good pinch chilli flakes

1–2 tbsp chopped herbs (I used sage and thyme)

Salt and pepper

Meatloaf may have got a bad name for itself over the years, but its humble appearance can mask a really fantastic slice of flavour.

Serves 6–8

Pre-heat the oven to 190°C. Oil a 23 cm x 13 cm non-stick loaf tin. Mix all the ingredients together. To take the guesswork out of it, fry a little blob of the mixture so you can taste it and adjust the seasoning. The Parmesan and sundried tomato paste are quite salty, but there's 1 kg of minced meats in there so it does need to be seasoned. But if you're confident enough, just chuck in some salt and pepper, pour, or rather, push the meat into the tin and then bake for about an hour. I cover it with foil at the beginning, cook it for about 40 minutes and then remove the foil for the last 20 minutes so that it can brown on top.

Cool slightly, turn out onto a platter, slice and serve with the sauce. Also delicious served cold the next day with a green salad and leftover tomato sauce.

crushed tomato sauce

Approx. 500 g cherry or vine tomatoes, cut in half

80 ml olive oil

3 cloves garlic, peeled and crushed

Big bunch chopped parsley, finely shopped

Salt and pepper

2 tbsp Dijon mustard

200 g black olives, roughly chopped

Few splashes Tabasco

1 tsp caster sugar

Roast the tomatoes with a splash of olive oil in the oven at least 30 minutes before the meatloaf has finished cooking. Roast them until slightly charring. Transfer to a bowl. Add in the rest of the ingredients and mix well but try not to break up the tomatoes too much. Taste, season and serve warm with the meatloaf.

30

oxtail stew

1 kg oxtail, cut into thick slices

3 red onions, peeled and sliced

2 tbsp olive oil

3-inch piece ginger, peeled and chopped

2 red chillies, deseeded and thinly sliced

3 cloves garlic, peeled and sliced

1 tbsp Chinese five-spice powder

800 g tinned chopped tomatoes

1 litre chicken or vegetable stock

50 ml fish sauce

50 ml soy sauce

3 good tbsp maple syrup (or honey)

Big bunch coriander, chopped

There is no need for too much seasoning in the early stages of this recipe as the end step adds a lot of flavour, so I have left out instructions to season prior to this. This is based on a Skye Gyngell recipe.

Serves 4–6

Put the oxtail in a saucepan and cover with cold water. Bring to the boil, simmer for 15 minutes, then drain and rinse with cold water. Set aside on a plate. Meanwhile, sauté the onion in the olive oil in a heavy-based saucepan until it just starts to colour. Add the ginger, chillies and garlic and then the Chinese five-spice powder. Turn up the heat, giving it a good blast, and mix well – this gets some colour onto the base of your stew. Turn down the heat and add the tomatoes and stock. Mix well, ensuring you don't have patches starting to burn, and bring up to a simmer.

Gently place the oxtail pieces in the sauce and mix well so they are well coated. Cook on a very gentle heat for about 1¹/₂ hours with a lid on. Stir and move them about or turn them over every 20 minutes or so, making sure it isn't burning and that they are well coated and subjected to heat evenly.

If it is burning, remove the oxtail pieces into a big dish and pour the sauce over them, but don't scrape the saucepan too harshly. Just let it drip onto to it so that the burnt stuff remains in the saucepan. Give the saucepan a good wash and then put everything back in and keep cooking. You can salvage a stew this way, but best to keep checking and monitoring what's going on to avoid this kind of rescue mission.

After 1¹/₂ hours, the oxtail should be pretty soft. Add in the fish sauce, soy and maple syrup or honey and mix well. Simmer for another 20 minutes or so. Taste and then leave it to rest for about an hour or overnight. This tastes better when it's had a chance to relax for a bit and then is reheated to order. Garnish with chopped coriander.

Recommend side: *Chargrilled broccoli with lemon, chilli and garlic (p. 248) or White bean and mushroom gratin (p. 256).*

31

veal escalopes with porcini dust and soft polenta

60 g dried porcini mushrooms

3 tsp flaky sea salt

Black pepper

8 veal escalopes
(about 90 g each)

500 ml milk

500 ml water (plus 2 stock cubes
– chicken or vegetable)

Olive oil

2–3 knobs butter

170 g polenta

80 g Parmesan, grated

2–3 tbsp Mascarpone

This dish is based on a few different recipes contained in the Donna Hay book, Fast, Fresh, Simple. *The 'porcini dust' is a fantastic thing to coat meat in and would also be lovely with pork or steak. The veal cooks in about 4 minutes, but you do need to be a bit generous with lashing the butter into the frying pan when it's cooking. Just a good knob per four escalopes.*

I serve it with some soft polenta, which uses a combination of milk and stock, and it actually works a treat, because you get the richness without the usual pounds of butter. I added a few spoons of mascarpone and some grated Parmesan, but even without these luxurious additions, when cooked with half milk, half stock, you get an impressive richness. Most packs of dried mushrooms are 20 g, so three packs are required. I would imagine all dried mushroom varieties will work for this.

Serves 4

If you have a spice grinder or small processor, it will make this much easier. Grind the mushrooms, salt and lots of pepper until it resembles a powder in parts with some chunky bits. This can take a while if your food processor is big – it just keeps whizzing around. Anyway, spread the porcini dust onto a large plate. Get the veal escalopes out of the fridge and bring them up to room temperature while you get the polenta ready.

In a heavy-based saucepan, bring the water, milk and stock cubes to the boil and then pour in the polenta and gradually whisk as it thickens up. It will bubble away like hot lava, so keep a lid partially over it and keep whisking. If it's getting too thick, chuck in a splash or two of water. Check the instructions on the polenta pack to see how long it needs to cook for. Some need 40 minutes of bubbling, some cook in ten. Either way, don't let it get too dry and remember it should be like smooth, very soft and slightly runny mash. Mix in the cheeses until well combined.

Heat the olive oil and a knob of butter till foaming and very hot and fry the escalopes on each side for a couple of minutes. Transfer to a warm plate and fry the rest. Serve with the polenta.

32

Italian beef stew

2 tbsp olive oil

1.5 kg diced beef, suitable for braising

2 onions, peeled and chopped

3 cloves garlic, peeled and crushed

1 bay leaf

2 good pinches salt

Freshly ground black pepper

1 tbsp tomato purée

250 ml red wine

500 g passata

Bunch sage and parsley, roughly chopped

This Italian stew has a robust tomato flavour and is one of those dishes that will taste better if it is made a day in advance and reheated – great if you're feeding a big group but are under pressure time-wise. Not surprisingly, it will work well with some mash, although it would also sit nicely on top of some pappardelle pasta. When buying the meat, do ask your butcher for beef that's suitable for braising or stewing.

Serves 4–6

Preheat the oven to 160°C. Heat the olive oil in a large casserole saucepan. When hot, fry the beef until brown. Keep the heat high – it will take 10–15 minutes to brown all of the meat. Add the onions, garlic and bay leaf and season well. Add the remaining ingredients except for the herbs, cover with a lid and cook in the oven for an hour.

Check the seasoning and cook for longer if the meat is still a bit tough. If the sauce is too liquidy, remove the lid and cook for another 30 minutes. At this stage, you can add the herbs for the final blast of cooking.

Recommended side: *Buttermilk and kale mash (p. 271).*

33

aubergine and feta meatballs

2 aubergines
50 ml olive oil
Salt and pepper
Pinch chilli flakes
Splash sherry or red wine
vinegar
2 cloves garlic
Pinch caster sugar
Big bunch flat-leaf parsley
Approx. 750–800 g minced beef
Approx. 200 g feta
Few lemon wedges

To serve:
Pita bread
Tzatziki
Mixed leaves

These meatballs are based on a Donna Hay recipe from her book, Seasons. Instead of roasting the aubergine, I sauté it to sharpen up the flavour with a splash of sherry vinegar, garlic and a pinch of chilli flakes. Make sure you let the aubergine cool down fully before mixing it with the mince and other herbs. If you don't, you'll find that it ruins the texture as it starts to cook the mince slightly, which is not only risky – unless you cook them straight away – but also not very pleasant texture-wise.

You can serve these straight from the oven with tzatziki, but they are also tasty when they have cooled down or even after a night in the fridge with some lemon juice on top. You can make instant tzatziki with a few spoons of Greek yoghurt, a clove of crushed garlic, finely diced cucumber and some dill, plus salt and pepper.

Makes about 30 balls (3 per person)

Dice the aubergines and fry in the olive oil over a high heat in a large non-stick pan. Season well and add the chilli flakes. When you have good colour on the aubergine, add the sherry vinegar, garlic and sugar. Keep cooking until you have good flavour and the mixture seems quite dry. Taste, adjust seasoning and then leave to cool fully.

Finely chop the parsley and mix with the mince and aubergine until well combined. Season the mince well and then crumble in the feta and mix until well blended. Then roll the mixture into golf-ball-sized balls and leave on a tray. The meatballs can be left overnight like this.

When you're ready to cook, preheat the oven to 190°C. Fry them in batches in olive oil in a non-stick frying pan until browned on a good portion of the surface area. Turn them over gently, as there is no egg to bind them. When well browned, transfer to a clean baking sheet and cook for about 12–15 minutes until piping hot and cooked through. Serve hot or cold, but either way a good squeeze of lemon juice brings them to life.

34

beef Wellington

4 tbsp olive oil

50 g butter

Salt, pepper and sprinkle caster sugar

Approx. 700–800 g fillet of beef, whole piece

1 onion, peeled and very finely chopped

Few sprigs thyme

4 garlic cloves, peeled and crushed

250 g button mushrooms, very finely diced

Splash cream

8–12 slices Parma ham

Approx. 250 g ready-made puff pastry

2 egg yolks, lightly beaten

The really well-seared-off meat in a beef Wellington works well with finely diced mushrooms sautéed with some onion and a splash of cream and cooked until very, very dry. Also, use an extremely generous amount of Parma ham to encase the entire lot, and a snug layer of all-butter puff pastry, the seams of which need a very good lick of egg yolk wash.

The tricky bit is getting the timing right for cooking the beef. If you have chilled the parcel down sufficiently in the fridge beforehand and it is very cold before it goes in the oven, the pastry will brown beautifully before the meat cooks too much inside. About 15 minutes in the oven at 190°C works, or when the pastry looks gorgeous and golden brown – then the chances are it's perfectly cooked inside. The lovely horseradish bread sauce goes nicely with the beef.

Serves 4

Heat half the olive oil and half the butter in a large frying pan or chargrill pan until very hot. Sprinkle the top of the beef with salt, pepper and a little sugar, and brown the meat, seasoned side down. Sprinkle some more seasoning onto the other surface, turn it over and sear the other side till you get plenty of charred colours without any real cooking taking place. Try to do this so that the beef is seasoned well and nicely caramelised on all sides. Remove it from the pan, let it cool down and refrigerate until ready to use.

Heat up the rest of the olive oil and butter and fry the onion till soft. Add the thyme, garlic and mushrooms. Cook on a high heat, as you want to cook the mushrooms until you end up with a very dry mixture. Add the cream, season and cook until the mixture is tasty and dry. Set aside to cool.

When the beef and mushrooms are cold, lay out 3 sheets of cling film – to give extra strength to your parcel – one on top of the other. Lay out a large 'blanket' of the slices of Parma ham and spread lightly with a layer of mushrooms. Place the beef in the centre and wrap up by rolling the cling film – almost as you would for rolling a Swiss roll – so that you end up with a tight 'log' shape. Twist the ends of the cling film to tighten to create a very tight log shape. Chill for a few hours.

When the pastry has defrosted, roll it into a ball and then roll it out quite thinly and cut into one neat rectangle. Remove the cling film and place the beef in the centre and trim away excess pastry so that the beef can be rolled and wrapped snugly. Brush a generous rim of the egg yolk onto the pastry and wrap the beef in the pastry, ensuring that mushrooms are not poking through any gaps. Cut away any excess pastry at the ends and use your fingers dipped in water to smooth out the seams and ensure the pastry is snug against the beef.

Then place the ugly, sealed side down onto a plate that you've lined with some greaseproof paper. Brush with egg yolk and chill until ready to bake. Heat oven to 190°C and preheat a non-stick baking sheet. Just before baking, lightly score the pastry with a sharp knife, but don't cut all the way through.

Cook the beef straight from the fridge – ugly side down – until the pastry is golden-brown and the beef medium-rare, which should take about 15 minutes. If you want it better done, just make sure the pastry doesn't burn: turn down the oven to 170°C and bake for an extra 5–10 minutes. When the pastry is a lovely golden brown, it should be perfect inside. Allow to rest for at least 8 minutes before carving.

horseradish bread sauce

1 horseradish, peeled and grated

5 slices white pan, roughly chopped

2 cloves garlic, peeled and crushed

2 good tsp English mustard

2 tsp caster sugar

100 ml olive oil

200 g crème fraîche

Salt

100 ml water

3 good tbsp white wine vinegar

Makes enough for 8–10 generous spoonfuls

Mix everything together in the blender until smooth. Season to taste. Serve warm or chilled. It will keep in the fridge for a few days.

35

veal steaks with Parma ham and blue cheese

400 g veal steak
2–4 slices Parma ham
Approx. 50–80 g blue cheese
Olive or rapeseed oil or butter
2 eggs
Flour
Salt and pepper

To serve:
Red onion
Spoonful of capers
Lemon juice
Mixed leaves

This veal dish really is extremely tasty with blue cheese, but you should feel free to change cheeses if you don't like it. Taleggio is a great creamy Italian cheese, but something thin and sharp would also work, as would some sort of stronger Swiss-style cheese. Indeed, a nice Irish cheese like Coolea, Glebe Brethan or even a mild Wicklow Brie would also work.

Serves 2

Tell your butcher you want to flatten out the veal steaks to make two giant escalopes that you're going to fold over and fry. If he or she is nice, they may even do this bit for you. If not, sandwich the veal in between sheets of cling film and bash with a rolling pin until it has at least doubled or tripled in size. On one half of the veal steak, lay down some Parma ham and then some blue cheese on top. Fold over and, using the cling film, flatten down and chill in the fridge until ready to cook. This is one of the few occasions that it's alright to cook meat straight from the fridge. (Normally it's better to bring meat to room temperature before you cook it, but because this is stuffed and the meat is exceptionally thin, you can cook it safely from cold.)

Preheat your oven to 180°C. Heat up some oil or butter in a decent frying pan and then dip the stuffed veal in the egg and then the flour. Season well and fry over high heat until nicely browned on both sides. You can continue to fry until cooked through, or you can transfer to the baking tray and bake for another 5–10 minutes so that the filling is piping hot and the veal very well done.

Make a little garnish by slicing the red onions very finely and soaking them in a squeeze of lemon juice and maybe a little drizzle of olive oil with salt and pepper. Mix in the capers and then mix with a few mixed leaves. It's just a sharp little side salad that balances nicely with the rich veal.

36

tile-makers' stew

4 tbsp olive oil

1 kg stewing beef, cut into decent-sized chunks

Salt

3 onions, peeled and sliced

4 cloves garlic, peeled and crushed

2 tbsp black peppercorns

2 tsp ground black pepper

2 bay leaves

250 ml red wine

400 g tin tomatoes

1 tube tomato purée

This Tuscan stew, known locally as peposo, *has a great story: it was made by the men stoking the ovens to bake the tiles for the roof of the cathedral in Florence. They'd leave a pot in corner of the tile oven and let the beef cook slowly as they worked, making a nourishing and tasty meal of affordable ingredients.*

Pepper is the star of the show in this recipe. It is interesting to note that manganese, vitamin K, copper, iron and fibre are all present in good quantities in 2 teaspoons of black pepper and this revered spice is also renowned for its carminative, diaphoretic and diuretic properties. The fact that black pepper is working so hard to create these chemical reactions in your body makes the vast quantities of it in this peposo *(peppery!) stew even more appealing. Be warned that kids may find this amount of pepper too much.*

Serves 4–6

In a large saucepan, with a tight-fitting lid, heat up the olive oil and brown the beef generously on all sides. Season with plenty of salt and then add the onions, garlic and peppercorns and cook for another 5–10 minutes until the onions have softened up and the mixture has shrunk down in size. Add the rest of the ingredients and then cover with a lid and cook very gently for about 2 hours, stirring every 20 or 30 minutes. Check the seasoning after 90 minutes and if you need to, add some water. You may want to remove the lid for the last 20–30 minutes of cooking time.

You can also put this in the oven and cook (with a tight-fitting lid) for 3–4 hours at 160°C until the beef is very tender and you have the desired consistency. Allow to cool slightly and serve, or else cool down and reheat the next day, when it will taste even better.

Recommended side: *Paprika and onion roast potatoes (p. 290).*

boozy venison stew

Good knob butter
4 tbsp olive oil
1 kg venison, diced
200 g bacon, diced
2 large onions, peeled and diced
4 sticks celery, diced
200 g button mushrooms, sliced
850 ml dark ale or stout
200 g stoned prunes, halved

Venison is a great choice for stews that are for a special treat or occasion. Not only does stewing bring out the tastiness of this naturally lean meat, but venison is also a rich source of iron. In this recipe, the gaminess of the meat is tamed and offset not only by the rich sweetness of the prunes, which almost melt in the cooking process, but also by the dark, hoppy beer it simmers in for the best part of $2^{1}/_{2}$ hours.

You could accompany it with some soothing, buttery mash, but a healthier option is to pair it with these roasted parsnips and carrots done in just a slick of olive oil and liberally sprinkled with seeds to add crunch and a hint of spice.

Serves 6–8

In a heavy saucepan, heat the butter and olive oil and sauté the venison over a medium heat in batches until brown, remove and set aside. In the same saucepan, fry the bacon and then add the onions and cook until soft, taking care not the burn them. Add the celery and mushrooms, stir, and then return the venison to the pan. Add the beer, drop the heat down to low, put the lid on, season well and cook for 2 hours.

Add the prunes and cook for another half hour until tender. You could serve this with the roasted parsnip and carrots, but a tasty alternative would be some celeriac mash or purée.

Recommended side: *Roast parsnips and carrots with fennel, honey and seeds (p. 258).*

38

meatballs with lemon and wine

500 g minced veal or beef
500 g minced pork
100 g breadcrumbs
1 egg
100 g Parmesan, grated
Salt and lots of black pepper
Few splashes of Worcestershire sauce
Big bunch parsley, finely chopped
3 cloves garlic, peeled and crushed
50 ml cream
Grated nutmeg (optional)

To finish
2 tbsp olive oil, in a bowl
$^1\!/_2$ bottle white wine
12 thin slices of lemon
4–6 bay leaves

These meatballs, which are based on ones in the Bocca Cookbook, are cooked in a delicious liquid enriched by a splash of cream, grated Parmesan and minced pork. I love the fact that they need no browning and have a very sophisticated flavour.

Serves 6

Preheat the oven to 220°C or even 250°C if you can. Mix all the ingredients for the meatballs together in a large bowl using a spatula. Don't be afraid to season well. Using oil to stop the meat sticking to your hands, divide and shape the meat into 12 balls. Have a shallow baking tray (non-stick if possible) ready to put them on. When you're done, wash your hands well and then bake the meatballs in your really hot oven for about 15 minutes.

Get a smaller gratin dish and oil it. When the meatballs are starting to colour, take them out and turn the oven down to 150°C. Transfer the meatballs very carefully, turning them over as you go. You want the meatballs to fit in nice and snug into the new gratin dish. Pour any juices from the shallow baking tray on top and then carefully pour in the white wine. Nestle in the bay leaves and top the meatballs with a slice of lemon. Bake uncovered for about 1$^1\!/_2$ hours, basting with the juices whenever you can.

Serve once they have cooled down a little – they need about 5 minutes to 'rest'. They are also lovely when reheated: pop them into the oven for about 20 minutes at 160°C once they've been brought to room temperature.

Recommended side: *Roast aubergine with curry yoghurt (p. 300).*

39

lamb cutlets with basil sauce

4–6 lamb cutlets, French trimmed

Few sprigs rosemary or thyme

50 g dried breadcrumbs

Salt and pepper

1 tbsp flour

1 egg

Olive oil

Butter

This is the perfect lamb dish, based on a Lucas Hollweg recipe, and will be happiness on a plate for people who love lamb and strong flavours. It's guaranteed to put a smile on your face.

Serves 2–3

You may have to give them a little scrape, but you should have lovely clean bones and a perfectly trimmed bit of lamb on each cutlet. Set aside. Chop up the rosemary or thyme and mix with the breadcrumbs and season well. If the breadcrumbs are a bit soft or too fresh, you can dry them out in a moderate oven at about 140°C for 10 minutes until dried out and slightly coloured.

This next bit is easy. Have a plate with the flour on it and season it well. Beat the egg and put it in a bowl. Dip the lamb cutlets into the flour and then into the egg and finally into the seasoned breadcrumbs. Heat the olive oil along with a good knob of butter and when good and hot, fry the cutlets on each side for about 5 minutes until nice and golden brown. Then put on a platter along with the sauce below and dig in!

basil sauce

1 egg yolk

1 clove garlic, peeled and crushed

2 tsp Dijon mustard

75 ml olive oil

Splash of anchovy essence or few squirts of Worcestershire sauce

1 tbsp red wine vinegar

Salt and pepper

Few basil leaves, very finely sliced

Few squirts Tabasco sauce

In a small bowl, mix the egg yolk along with the garlic clove and the mustard. It will form the base to which you slowly add and whisk in a few drops of olive oil. Continue in a thin stream and you should feel it start to thicken. Add about half the olive oil and then season with the anchovy essence and the red wine vinegar. Then start adding the rest of the oil, which will thicken it up a bit more. Season really well and add the basil leaves and Tabasco. Taste and adjust the seasoning; you can tone it down by adding 25 ml of a lighter olive oil. You can make this a few hours ahead of time and keep in the fridge until ready to serve.

lamb skewers with pistachio aioli

500 g minced lamb

Good pinch salt and ground black pepper

2 cloves garlic, peeled and crushed

Small bit of olive oil in a bowl or saucer

4–6 rosemary stalks (or soaked wooden skewers or metal ones)

The lamb skewers were very easy to prepare and the pistachio aioli is wonderful. The quantity below will make more than you need, but hang on to it so that you can slather it on all sorts of fish and chicken or even just to put on boiled potatoes.

Serves 4 as a starter or part of large buffet

Mix the lamb, salt, pepper and garlic. Then mould an equal amount of meat on the skewers or stalks using your hands that you should dip into the oil. Then put them all on a plate, cover them and chill in the fridge until ready to cook. When you are ready, heat up a bit more olive oil in a large non-stick frying pan and when it's nearly smoking, fry the skewers on each side until good and brown. You want them to form a good, dark crust so that they will stay fixed onto the skewers. Turn them over in the pan and shake them gently. You don't want to manhandle them but rather coax them into cooking on all sides. Put on a large platter or individual plates with some of the aioli and mixed leaves.

pistachio aioli

110 g shelled pistachios

Big bunch parsley

2 tsp olive oil

2 tbsp capers

1 egg yolk

3 cloves garlic, peeled and crushed

100 ml olive oil

Juice of 1 lemon

Splash sherry vinegar

Small squeeze agave syrup or honey

Salt and pepper

Extra 50 ml olive oil or water

On pulse mode, whizz the pistachios and parsley until they form a coarse and slightly chunky crumb. Add the 2 teaspoons of olive oil and the capers and give it one final blitz. Once you have an even crumb, leave it in the food processor.

In a bowl, whisk the egg yolk with the garlic and then very slowly start adding the olive oil until you can feel it emulsifying. Then you can add this a bit more steadily. Once you are at the halfway point of adding the 100 ml olive oil, mix in the lemon juice and then continue with the rest of the oil. Then add this to the ground-up pistachios along with the splash of sherry vinegar, squeeze of agave and some salt and pepper. Process and then you can add either another 50 ml of olive oil or water, depending on how loose or rich you want to keep it. Do this until you get the desired consistency, but taste and adjust the seasoning. You may need to add more lemon juice, sherry vinegar or salt. Refrigerate until ready to use.

41

lamb stir-fry

2 cannons of lamb, sliced

Salt and pepper

1 tsp cornstarch

1 tbsp olive oil

1 tsp cumin seeds

1 tsp chilli powder

2-inch piece ginger, peeled and sliced

3 cloves garlic

400 g tinned chickpeas, rinsed and drained

Big bunch coriander, roughly chopped

Big bunch spring onions

The lamb stir-fry, made with cannon of lamb, which is taken from the loin of lamb so is very lean – a bit like fillet steak. It can also be quite expensive, but can sometimes be had at a decent price. According to some nutritionists, lamb is gentle on the digestion, yet full of flavour, and the cumin, chilli, ginger and garlic make it warming but not too overwhelming, as they (and all that drab colour) are brightened up by the chickpeas, coriander and spring onion. A lovely dish to warm you up on a cool winter's night.

Serves 3–4

In a bowl, toss the lamb with some salt and pepper, the cornstarch, oil, spices, ginger and garlic and leave to marinate for about half an hour. Scatter the chickpeas on a large plate and sprinkle the coriander and chopped spring onions over them. Then stir-fry the lamb for about 7–10 minutes and when done to your liking, arrange on top of the chickpeas and serve.

42

lamb rendang

1 tbsp coconut or olive oil

1 onion, peeled and chopped

2 kg diced stewing lamb

400 ml coconut milk

Salt and pepper

1 tbsp coriander seeds

3-inch piece ginger, peeled and chopped

8 cloves garlic, peeled and finely chopped

1 green chilli, chopped (seeds and all)

2 stalks lemongrass with outer leaves removed, finely chopped

1 tbsp black mustard seeds

1 tbsp yellow mustard seeds

As the ingredients list for curries can often be pretty long, cooking one from scratch is not something many of us choose to do on a regular basis. It can seem, well, a bit of a chore in comparison to picking up the phone and ordering one. But with curries, the more you put in in terms of time and quality dried spices that are fresh, the better they are. This rendang has the virtue of tasting like you've taken great care, but in reality everything is strewn on top of the lamb and onion and the whole thing left to stew. It couldn't be simpler – more assembly than alchemy – and it tastes sensational. You don't even have to brown the meat, which really is lazy cooking. It is lovely with plain basmati rice, perhaps sprinkled with chopped coriander, or even just some naan and a lovely green salad.

Serves 8–10

Sweat the onion in oil until it gets soft – about 7 minutes. Then add the lamb and everything else in one go and cook for about 2 hours over a low to medium heat, with the lid on. Remove the lid for the final 20–30 minutes to allow the moisture to evaporate and the sauce to thicken. The lamb may be tender enough after 90 minutes, but it may need longer.

Add a bit of water if it starts to dry out too much. You may worry that one tin of coconut milk isn't enough, but it's usually plenty as the dish cooks down, as long as the lid stays on.

lamb and quinoa kofte

100 g quinoa
Bunch parsley
Bunch dill
Bunch coriander
1 tsp cumin seeds
1 tsp fennel seeds
Good pinch chilli flakes
500 g minced lamb
2 tbsp soy sauce
Salt and pepper
Anchovy and olive sauce

For the sauce:
Small tin anchovy fillets
4 cloves garlic, peeled and crushed
Approx. 50 g green, stoned olives
Bunch mint
50 ml olive oil
Juice of 1 lemon

Middle Eastern cooking is very versatile and can often be the best option when you have a bunch of people with different tastes to cater for. This lamb and quinoa kofte dish, adapted from a Peter Gordon recipe, is fabulous and the accompanying olive and anchovy sauce is bursting with umami flavours that will also be tasty on falafels.

Serves 4 (2 kofte per person)

Cook the quinoa in boiling water for about 10 minutes and then drain and allow to cool. You can blitz the herbs in a food processor or else chop by hand. Chuck all the ingredients for the kofte in a bowl and mix really well. It may be easier to do this with your hands. Have a little bowl of olive oil handy, so that you can oil your hands and then shape the mixture into cigar shapes (about 8 in total) and lay them on a baking tray and stick them in the fridge until you are ready to cook. It's ideal if you can leave them in there for about an hour. You can cook these by frying them in some olive oil, or you could bake them for about 25–30 minutes at 180°C. They don't take long to cook, but a little charring goes a long way in terms of flavour.

Blitz all the ingredients for the sauce together in a food processor (or mix and chop everything by hand) and season to taste.

Recommended side: *Carrot salad with ginger and lemon (p.254).*

44

lamb and chickpea soupy stew

2 tbsp olive oil

2 onions, peeled and chopped

4 garlic cloves, peeled and
chopped

600 g diced lamb shoulder

Salt and pepper

2 tsp ground cumin

1 tsp paprika

¹/₂ tsp ground cloves

2 bay leaves

2–3 tbsp tomato purée

1 litre chicken stock

1200 g tinned chickpeas

800 g tinned tomatoes

Bunch coriander, chopped

Black olives

The combination of cloves and paprika works a treat in this lamb dish. Lamb shoulder is good as it is relatively cheap. However, it can be quite fatty, so trim it well or ask the butcher to give you something leaner for braising. Pork or beef would also work really well in this stew, although the lamb always seems to go so well with chickpeas. If you want a vegetarian option, replace the lamb with 2–3 sweet potatoes chopped into small chunks. Cook for about an hour instead of three!

Serves 4–6

Heat the olive oil in a big saucepan, for which you have a lid. Sweat the onions and garlic for 5 minutes until they go soft, then turn up the heat and put in the lamb. Brown the meat, but try not to let the mixture burn. Season well then add in the cumin, paprika, cloves and bay leaves. Mix well so the spices coat all the lamb. Add in the tomato purée, mix well then add in the stock, chickpeas and tomatoes. Put the lid on and cook for about 3 hours over a very gentle heat. You may need to add water during cooking. Taste and adjust the seasoning. Garnish with coriander and olives, and serve with bread and salad.

roast shoulder of lamb

1.6 kg lamb shoulder on the bone

2 heads of garlic

Big handful rosemary

Olive oil

Salt and pepper

This very simple method for cooking lamb comes from Geoff Lenehan, brother of restaurateur Maisha Lenehan, and is truly delicious. Yes, it has rosemary and garlic like lots of other roast lamb dishes, but for good reason: they taste great together. If you have any lamb leftover, use it for the lamb salad. I'll often roast two of them to ensure there are plenty of leftovers.

Serves 4

Preheat the oven to 220°C. Place the lamb on a large sheet of tin foil and then in a roasting tin. Cut the garlic heads horizontally and put into the lamb parcel along with some rosemary, a good drizzle of olive oil and seasoning. Wrap up in the tin foil and cook for 30 minutes on a high heat, then turn down the oven to 170°C and cook for another $3^1/_2$ to 4 hours.

Allow to cool slightly and serve slices of lamb with your favourite potato dish.

Recommended side: *Balsamic potatoes (p. 274).*

46

roast lamb salad

Leftover lamb
Few splashes soy sauce
Sprinkle sesame seeds

For the dressing:
1 tbsp soy sauce
1 tbsp English mustard
1 tsp sugar
Juice of 2 limes
2 cloves garlic, peeled and crushed
1 tbsp smooth peanut butter
1 tsp tahini
1 tbsp sweet chilli sauce
3 tbsp mayonnaise
1 green chilli
3 tbsp vinegar

For the salad:
Bunch mâche (lamb's lettuce)
Few heads baby gem lettuce
1 cucumber
Bunch spring onions, chopped
1 red onion, peeled and sliced
Bunch coriander and mint

You will often have shards of lamb leftover after roasting a leg or shoulder of lamb, and this is an ideal way to serve them.

Whizz all the ingredients together for the dressing. Add some hot water if it's too thick. Check the seasoning and adjust as necessary.

Heat up your grill and place shards of lamb on a baking tray. Sprinkle with some soy sauce and sesame seeds. It is usually fatty enough, so you shouldn't need any olive oil. But if it looks a bit dry, give it a splash of olive oil. Grill for 5–10 minutes till starting to char.

Mix the salad ingredients together with some dressing and top with hot, grilled lamb. Serve straight away.

47

stuffed shoulder of lamb

1 lamb shoulder, boned
(approx. 2.3 kg)

2 tbsp dried oregano

Salt and pepper

Olive oil

2 lemons, cut in half

Sprigs thyme and rosemary

1 onion, cut into quarters

1 head garlic, cut in half,
horizontally

For the stuffing:

Olive oil

1 onion, peeled and very finely
diced

2 cloves garlic, peeled and
chopped

500 g sausage meat

1 big handful Swiss chard or
spinach, chopped

100 g breadcrumbs

Thyme and/or rosemary
(optional)

Garlic, minced (optional)

This is the perfect Sunday lunch dish, as it lends a real sense of occasion to the day and makes you think of those formal lunches of our youth. I use Ed Hick's gourmet sausages in the stuffing. You'll need some butcher's string for this.

Serves 6

Marinate the lamb with the oregano, pepper, salt, good few glugs of olive oil and lemons (the juice of which you can squeeze on to the lamb) in a big roasting tray or similar. Add the thyme and rosemary. You'll add the onion and garlic to the roasting tin just before it goes into the oven. Leave the rest of it to marinate for a few hours somewhere cool or leave it out for about an hour at room temperature while you make the stuffing and let it cool down.

To make the stuffing, sweat the onion and garlic in lots of olive oil and then turn up the heat and add the sausage meat, which you'll have to break up with a wooden spoon as it cooks. This will take a while – don't be afraid of pushing and shoving this around so you start to get some even colour. At this stage, add the Swiss chard or spinach. If it's very tough and unruly, you could cook it in boiling water for about 30 seconds, drain, rinse, dry and chop. But it should wilt down sufficiently. Add in the breadcrumbs and stir well – this is easier to do in a big bowl. Mix it well, taste and adjust the seasoning. Also, feel free to add some chopped thyme and rosemary or loads more garlic. Allow it to cool down properly before stuffing the lamb, though.

Then lay the boned lamb shoulder out as flat as you can, into a vaguely rectangular shape – you're going to be making a sort of roll of it. Cut the string into about 6 or 8 lengths that are long enough to tie around the lamb. Slip them under the lamb so that all you've left to do is spoon stuffing in a line along the lamb and then pull each string and tie snugly at the top. Eventually you will create something that looks like a boned and rolled loin of something or other. Put in the roasting tin along with the onion and garlic. Season more and roast at 180°C for about 30 minutes. Then turn down the oven, cover with foil and roast for another 2 hours at 150°C. Baste whenever you can, and if you want, add a glass of white wine to the roasting tin. Allow the meat to rest for about 15 minutes before slicing and serving.

roast shoulder of lamb with onions and potatoes

6 large white onions, very thinly sliced

50 ml olive oil

1 bottle white wine

Salt and pepper

1 shoulder of lamb, on the bone

Big knob butter

15 cloves garlic

4 big sprigs rosemary

Few leaves sage

Few sprigs thyme

Water or stock as required

4 large potatoes, diced

This is a really tasty way to do shoulder of lamb and has the added benefits of ready-made gravy and ready-to-go roast spuds. Slow cooking a tough piece of meat means the connective tissues are able to break down, but it does require liquid to do this. Ideally the heat will be gentle enough to ensure it doesn't all leak out into the roasting tin, but remains within the meat, guaranteeing each mouthful stays tender and juicy rather than dry and stringy. Having the oven at about 140°C for 3–4 hours helps this process, but the meat needs to be well covered in foil. Chuck in the spuds about 1 hour before the end of the allotted cooking time. They end up roasting and absorbing some of the delicious brown juices which in turn, help them caramelise and turn all meaty. The onions slowly melt away to resemble something you'd find swimming around the most delicious French onion soup.

Serves 4

Put the onions in a large roasting tray and pour over the olive oil and wine. Season really well and then put the lamb shoulder on top of the onions. Rub with the butter and season. Scatter the garlic and herbs on top of and around the lamb. Cover really well with tinfoil and roast for 3 hours. Check every now and then and turn over. Add more water or stock or even some more wine if the pan is drying out. After 3 hours, add the spuds and spoon over some of the oils and juices on to them. Roast for another hour without the foil on to let the lamb colour and the spuds caramelise in parts and cook gently. Allow to rest for about 10 minutes before slicing and serving with spoonfuls of delicious melted onions and roast potatoes.

49

lamb with capers, parsley and anchovies

2 onions, peeled and very finely chopped

2 cloves garlic, peeled and crushed

75 g butter

80 g breadcrumbs

40 g capers

Big bunch flat-leaf parsley, roughly chopped

Juice of 1 lemon

Few glugs olive oil

1 boned leg of lamb

Salt and pepper

1 small tin anchovies

Few sprigs rosemary

100 ml white wine

300 ml chicken stock

2 tbsp redcurrant jelly

This recipe has been adapted from a Diana Henry one, which I've doctored even further by adding some anchovies to the lamb when roasting. Anchovies have that fantastic umami quality to them with none of the fishiness you might expect. The ones in small tins – once drained of excess oil – can be slipped into sauces or anything that needs to be beefed up and you don't even need to tell anyone. They will just wonder what that fabulous piquancy is in all your dishes. This recipe uses a boned leg of lamb but you could ask the butcher to butterfly it out a bit. You need some twine but tell your butcher that you want to stuff it, roll it up and tie it and let them flatten it out for you to make this easier.

Serves 6

Preheat the oven to 220°C. Sweat together the onions, garlic and butter together in a heavy-based saucepan till nice and soft. Then throw in the breadcrumbs, capers, parsley, lemon juice and olive oil. Season with plenty of black pepper and some salt. The stuffing should be able to hold its own shape and not be too wet. If it's too dry, add some more lemon juice and olive oil.

Spread out the lamb, season it up, stuff it, roll it up and tie it together until it resembles a log. Put it in a roasting tin, drape the anchovies over it, season with more salt and pepper, olive oil and some sprigs of rosemary.

Cook at 220°C for about 15 minutes, then cover with foil and reduce the temperature to 150°C and cook for about 45 minutes to an hour. Leave to rest somewhere warm and then deglaze the pan with some wine, then pour into a little saucepan and let it simmer away.

Add the stock and redcurrant jelly. Reduce down until it becomes a bit more syrupy, taste and adjust seasoning. If you find it tastes great but is too watery then add a small amount of cornflour which you mix with cold water. This should thicken it up nicely. Once the meat has rested, slice and serve with a splash of gravy.

Recommended side: *Jewelled couscous (p. 299).*

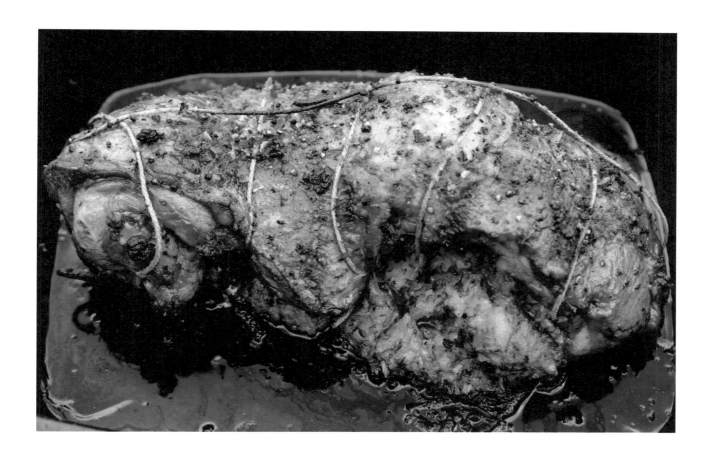

lamb two ways

1 bunch mint

1 bunch parsley

3 cloves garlic, peeled

Juice and zest of 2 lemons

Good squeeze honey

1 small tin anchovies

Black pepper

100 ml olive oil

1–2 tbsp rosemary leaves

I leg of lamb, butterflied

This barbecued or roast leg of lamb can also be turned into a gorgeous warm roast lamb salad.

Mix everything in your food processor, except for the lamb itself. Then marinate the leg of lamb in the mixture, preferably overnight. This can then be cooked either on a barbecue or in a really hot oven so that you char and roast the outside really well (at about 220°C for about 18 minutes). It's better to bring the lamb to room temperature before you cook it, ideally for about an hour. When you've let it rest, carve into thin slices and either serve as is or make a large platter of salad with the ingredients on p. 98.

51

warm lamb salad

Serves 8

About 8 good handfuls of mixed
leaves or approx. 600 g

Extra olive oil, lemon juice or
splash balsamic vinegar

Bunch basil, chopped

Bunch mint, chopped

Bunch parsley, chopped

200 g feta, diced

1 red onion, thinly sliced

Roast leg of lamb, sliced

2 tbsp pine nuts, lightly toasted

Toss the mixed leaves with some olive oil and splash of lemon juice or
balsamic and then lay out on a large platter. Sprinkle the herbs and feta
on top, then the red onions, lamb and pine nuts and let everyone help
themselves.

52

Sicilian lamb stew

2 onions peeled and thinly
sliced

3–4 tbsp olive oil

5 slices smoked streaky bacon,
diced

1 kg boneless lamb shoulder,
diced

Salt and pepper

3 cloves garlic, peeled and
chopped

250 ml red wine

250 ml water/stock

450 g baby new potatoes

200 g Pecorino, diced

*This Sicilian lamb stew originally comes from one of my favourite books, The
Cook's Book, edited by Jill Norman. The idea of serving a lamb stew for lunch or
brunch may seem a bit odd, but the fact that it is such a delicious, rich, meaty stew
under a dotted blanket of Pecorino cheese made it seem more of a daytime dish
than an evening one. It is a complete one-pot wonder, as you simply throw some
potatoes in there too.*

Serves 6

Preheat the oven to 160°C. Sweat the onions in half the olive oil for about
8–10 minutes in a heavy based saucepan with a lid. Turn up the heat and add
the bacon and allow the onions to brown a bit and the bacon to caramelise.
When that's done, remove the bacon and onions onto a plate for a few
minutes while you brown the lamb in the rest of the olive oil over a high heat.
Season well and really keep this going till you have good patches of brown on
the lamb chunks. Add the onions and bacon back into the pan, add the garlic
and wine and simmer to reduce by half.

Then add the water or stock and potatoes. Bring up to the boil, and then
put in the oven with the lid on for 45 minutes. Taste to make sure it's well
seasoned and then cook for another 45 minutes. Taste again to make sure you
are happy with the flavour, consistency and tenderness of the lamb. If it's too
tough, add some more stock and water and cook for another 20 minutes. Add
the cheese 10 minutes before the end so it has a chance to melt. Remove from
the oven and let it rest for a while before serving in big bowls.

53

Six Nations stew

3 kg diced lamb

Olive oil

Salt and pepper

6 red onions, finely sliced

3 tsp Chinese five-spice powder

3-inch piece ginger, peeled and grated

1 head garlic, peeled and sliced

2–3 tbsp harissa (optional)

1.5 litres stock

1600 g tinned tomatoes

4 bay leaves

400 g stoned prunes

50 ml soy sauce

50 ml maple syrup

As the name suggests, this is a great dish for serving to a bunch of people watching a match on television. It's easy to prepare – maybe even do it the day before – and is not too spicy or rich so will suit kids too. It's actually a hybrid of two of my older recipes, but cuts down on the spices and uses lamb instead of oxtail. This will also taste great the next day, but great to do in bulk and then freeze for best-ever ready meals. Simply allow to thaw out overnight in the fridge and then heat up gently in a saucepan until simmering hot and bubbling for at least 5–10 minutes. You may have to add some water to get it going as the freezer always dries it up. It is lovely to serve with sweet potato purée.

Serves up to 12

In a large frying pan, cook the lamb in batches in olive oil, season well and set aside. In another large heavy-based saucepan (or even use two) sweat the onions in some olive oil until soft. Add the five-spice powder, ginger, garlic and harissa to the onions and mix well. Cook out for another few minutes. When the lamb is all done, add to the saucepan, mix well and deglaze the frying pan with some of the stock and pour it into the saucepan. Add the tinned tomatoes and bay leaves along with the rest of the stock. Mix well and bring up to the boil, then simmer for about 1¹/₂ hours.

Keep the lid on at first but remove it after about an hour so it can reduce and thicken up. Stir occasionally and then add the prunes, soy sauce and maple syrup. Cook for another 20 minutes and then cool slightly and taste. Adjust the seasoning as necessary.

54

crisp shredded lamb

4 lamb shanks
At least 2.5 litres chicken stock
Sprigs rosemary
Olive oil
Salt and pepper
Pinch chilli flakes
1–2 tsp mild curry powder
Squeeze honey

This lamb dish is inspired by the wonderful Heston Blumenthal, though without a lot of the superchef elements. It gets a final bit of roasting and grilling that gives the lamb a crisp, caramelized edge that makes it moreish. The end result resembles the crispy duck you get in Chinese restaurants, but not as fatty and much tastier.

If you have any leftover, I heartily recommend adding it to the giant couscous salad (p. 282) or serving as part of the lamb salad (p. 98).

Serves 6–8, possibly 10

In a large saucepan with a lid, cook the lamb shanks in the chicken stock with the rosemary and bring up to gentle simmer and cook on the stove for at least 3 hours. You can turn them over every 30 minutes or so, making sure they are well submerged. If you need to add more water, then do. You can also skim away any 'scum' that appears on the surface. Making sure it is gently simmering rather than boiling rapidly will help this. The meat should pull away with absolutely no effort when it's cooked, so let nature and cooking take their course. When the meat is genuinely falling off the bones, let them settle down and cool a little. Then remove them to a large roasting pan, discard the stock and shred the meat off the bone using a fork. You can discard any really fatty bits, but you will be amazed how much meat there is.

Drizzle the lamb generously with olive oil, some salt and pepper, chilli flakes, curry powder and a good squeeze of honey. Toss and mix around in the roasting tin. You can let it cool down at this stage and then refrigerate overnight, or keep going by preheating oven to 200°C and roasting it for about 20 minutes or so uncovered. You'll have to remove it from the oven and mix it around so that it crisps up evenly. You may well find your grill is helpful and that adding more honey will crisp and caramelise it even further. Just remember to balance out the sweetness with some salt and pepper and maybe some garlic.

Serve warm in a big bowl alongside a salad or mix it up with some cooked giant couscous salad, to which you've added some pomegranate seeds and lots of herbs.

Recommended side: *Giant couscous salad (p. 282).*

55

lamb hot pot with harissa yoghurt

Approx. 70 ml olive oil

400 g diced lamb

Salt and pepper

2 large Spanish onions, peeled and sliced

6 cloves garlic, peeled and sliced

1 red chilli, sliced

1 tsp ground cumin

$1/2$ tsp ground cinnamon

$1/2$ tsp ground coriander

$1/2$ tsp caraway seeds

Good pinch saffron

$1/2$ celeriac, peeled and chopped

2 carrots, peeled and sliced

3 sticks celery, sliced

400 g tinned tomatoes

2 litres of water or vegetable stock

100 g pearl barley

50 g Puy lentils

400 g tinned chickpeas

Big bunch parsley, chopped

Approx. 250 g plain Greek yoghurt

1 tbsp harissa paste

1 tbsp good tomato chutney

The hot pot is a fabulous thing to come home to. Like most stews, this lamb hot pot with harissa yoghurt tastes better the next day, so get it over and done with today, leave overnight and then reheat for tomorrow. This is delicious with some good bread and a glass of something red and strong.

Serves 6

Heat the oil in a large heavy-bottomed saucepan and brown the lamb and season well. Add the onion, garlic and chilli and cook for another few minutes with a lid on until soft. Add the spices including the saffron and stir well and get some good colour on everything. Then add the vegetables and tomatoes and stock, as well as the barley and lentils, put a lid on it and simmer for at least 1 hour. Check to see how tender the lamb is and season; if you need to cook for longer, give it another 30 minutes. When you are happy the lamb is tender enough, add in the tinned chickpeas and chopped parsley and cook for another few minutes. Mix the yoghurt with some harissa and the tomato chutney and spoon on top of each serving.

56

honey and fennel roast shoulder of lamb

1 shoulder of lamb
1 head garlic, left whole, skin on
2 tsp fennel seeds
Squeeze of honey
Salt and pepper

A roast shoulder on a Sunday, served with gravy and roast spuds, will usually mean enough leftovers for the next day, which is perfect for scavenging children just home from school and pleading for grub or for anyone who prefers to bring lunch into work rather than buy another overpriced, underwhelming sandwich.

For a simple roast dinner, serve with crispy potatoes, roasted carrots and parsnips and gravy. But to plan ahead, you could always do a second one so you have enough for the salad below.

Serves 4

Preheat the oven to 180°C degrees. Wrap the joint tightly in tinfoil – two layers if you can – and place in a roasting tin and roast for 3–4 hours until it's falling away from the bone. Halfway through cooking, take it out of the oven and turn the joint over. Season well with salt, pepper, the honey and fennel seeds, and then place it back in the roasting tin with the head of garlic.

When it's done, let it cool, remove the bone and shred the meat, which will have a moreish caramelised finish in places. If it's too fatty at this stage, put it back in the oven for another 40 minutes or so without foil to let the fat render off.

57

leftover lamb and chickpea salad

400 g tinned chickpeas, drained
and rinsed

Olive oil

Salt and pepper

1 tsp fennel seeds

1 tsp cumin seeds

Roast shoulder of lamb,
shredded

1 Chinese cabbage, finely sliced

1 yellow pepper, finely sliced

200 g feta, roughly broken into
cubes

For the dressing:

100 ml olive oil

2 tbsp sherry vinegar

2–3 tbsp honey

Salt and pepper

Large bunch mint, finely
chopped

This is my favourite type of food. The roasted joint is delicious on its own, but it also produced enough meat for this toothsome, crunchy salad. But a salad is just one option. Try a lamb wrap with tzatziki, lettuce and harissa or flake it over toasted sourdough with mayo, chipotle paste, sliced tomato and coriander. The variations are endless.

Serves 4–6

Preheat the oven to 200°C degrees. Toast the chickpeas on a tray in the oven for about 15 minutes with a little olive oil, some salt and pepper, and the fennel and cumin seeds. Leave aside to cool.

Make the dressing by mixing all the ingredients together and adding the finely chopped mint at the end. To assemble the salad, toss all the ingredients together with the dressing.

58

pork fillet with prunes and cream sauce

12 soft prunes, chopped into quarters

250 ml white wine

600 g pork tenderloin (approx. one big one)

1 tbsp flour

Salt and pepper

3 tbsp olive oil

Knob butter

2 leeks, finely sliced

2 cloves garlic, peeled and chopped

250 ml cream

Bunch tarragon, chopped

This is a hearty and comforting dish that is quick enough to prepare, using classic techniques and a little flair.

Serves 4

Soak the prunes in the wine while you get everything else sorted. Cut the pork into 1 cm thick slices and dust with the flour and season well. Heat up the olive oil until just about smoking and fry the pork until golden brown on both sides. Remove the pork into a bowl and then add a knob of butter and fry the leeks until they are soft. Add the garlic, and then the wine and prunes, which will also help deglaze the pan. Reduce the liquid significantly, then add the cream and the pork. Mix well and cook through for about 5 minutes. Then add the tarragon and check the seasoning. Simple but very tasty.

Recommended side: *Leek and bread pudding (p. 298).*

59

buckwheat noodles with black pudding, shiitake and bok choy

200 g black pudding

1 tsp olive oil

1 tsp sesame oil

1 small red onion, peeled and diced

2-inch piece ginger, peeled and chopped

1 clove garlic, peeled and crushed

Pinch chilli flakes

8–12 shiitake mushrooms, sliced

50 ml soy sauce

50 ml mirin

2 bok choy, sliced

400 g buckwheat noodles

2 tbsp peanuts, lightly toasted

Peter Gordon's cookbook Fusion: A Culinary Journey *often inspires creativity, as it's full of interesting combinations. The buckwheat noodles and black pudding in this recipe make an unbelievably umami and moreish Asian-Irish dish, which is very tasty. You could 'green it up' by adding things like peas and more baby spinach, but the bok choy is probably sufficient.*

Serves 4

Remove the black pudding meat from its casing and crumble into a hot frying pan. Cook gently until crisp in parts, then put the pudding into a bowl. Using the same saucepan, heat the olive oil and sesame oil. Sweat the onion for a few minutes along with the ginger, garlic and chilli.

Then return the crumbled and cooked black pudding to the pan, along with the mushrooms. Turn up the heat and get some colour going. Just when you think it all needs to cool off, add in the soy sauce and mirin. Let it sizzle and reduce for a minute and then add the bok choy and let the heat wilt it slightly.

Leave off the heat while you cook the noodles in boiling water as instructed on the packet. Drain the noodles and toss with a little extra olive oil to stop them sticking. Toast the peanuts in a dry pan and crush slightly. Serve in individual bowls. Meanwhile, give the pudding mixture a final sizzle and spoon some on top along with the peanuts or else toss the whole lot together and serve.

60

baked beans with chorizo, egg and feta

Splash olive oil

1 chorizo sausage, diced

2 onions, peeled and finely chopped

4 garlic cloves peeled and finely chopped

Few sprigs thyme or rosemary

80 ml red wine vinegar

4 tbsp tomato purée

Salt and pepper

400 g tinned cannellini beans, drained and rinsed

4 large eggs

200 g pack of feta (approx.)

This amazingly tasty recipe comes from Australian chef Karen Martini. It is a convenient supper dish that would also be perfect for brunch. Ingredients like feta and chorizo make everything taste good, as they are so tasty themselves. Combining them with the plainer flavours of the beans and eggs works really well – tasty and very comforting. You can serve with bread and a salad if you want some healthy greens.

Serves 4

Preheat the oven to 180°C. Heat the olive oil in a large frying pan or saucepan and sauté the chorizo in a little olive oil until it starts to caramelise. It does release lots of fat, which you can drain out if you're being good, or leave in for extra unctuousness. Add the onions and continue to sauté until they too are just starting to colour. Add the garlic, herbs, red wine vinegar, tomato purée and 3 tablespoons of water. Mix well, season and cook for another few minutes.

When everything feels well blended, take off the heat, mix in the cannellini beans and then transfer to a gratin dish of some sort. Make four 'wells' or 'holes' in the beans and crack an egg into each one. Drizzle with more olive oil, crumble the feta on top, season with lots of black pepper and bake for 15 minutes or so until the eggs are just cooked.

61

pork and lettuce parcels

500 g minced pork

1 onion, peeled and finely chopped

3 garlic cloves, peeled and crushed

2 sticks lemongrass, very finely chopped

2 teaspoons cornflour

1 bunch mint, finely chopped

1 bunch coriander, finely chopped

50 ml fish sauce

2 tbsp caster sugar

Few heads baby gem lettuce

1 cucumber, peeled

1 red onion, finely sliced

Splash chilli sauce

Coriander and mint, chopped, to serve

Juice of 1–2 limes

This uses minced pork so you should ask your butcher to mince some for you. It works very nicely as a starter, though with some accompaniments, it could easily work as a main course too.

Perfect as a starter for 4–6

Preheat the oven to 200°C. Mix all the ingredients together and then roll into little balls and place on an oiled baking tray. Bake for 15–20 minutes. You may want to shake them around during cooking as they tend to burn and stick because of the sugar. Meanwhile, you can make little salad boats to serve them in.

To make the garnish, wash and separate a few heads of baby gem lettuce. Grate a cucumber without the skin and mix with a finely sliced red onion. Add a splash of sweet chilli sauce and some extra coriander and mint. Add the juice of a lime or two, and that's it!

62

pork schnitzel

Salt and pepper

2 eggs, beaten

1 clove garlic, peeled and crushed

$^1/_2$ tsp smoked sweet paprika

1 tsp dried oregano (or thyme)

1 trimmed pork tenderloin, cut into 2 cm thick slices

100 g breadcrumbs

Sunflower or rapeseed oil

Good few knobs butter

Lemon wedges to serve

Everyone seems to like wiener schnitzel or veal alla milanese. It could be the breadcrumbs, or the thinness of the meat, or just the fact that it's basically good, old-fashioned fried food. These schnitzels are great with some buttered noodles, a squeeze of lemon juice or even some celeriac remoulade and a green salad.

Serves 4

Preheat the oven to 180°C. Season the eggs and add the garlic, paprika, dried herbs and whisk well. Put the slices of pork between two sheets of cling film (or in a heavy-duty Ziploc lunch bag) and bash with a rolling pin until nearly doubled in size. When they are all done, drop the pork into the seasoned egg mixture. Wash your cutting boards and utensils carefully and get a plate or tray of breadcrumbs set up. You can do this step up to 12 hours in advance.

When you are ready for final cooking, heat the oil in a large frying pan and add a knob of butter. Then remove a couple of pieces of pork from the egg mixture and dip the pork into the breadcrumbs. Press them into the breadcrumbs so that they stick well, and then fry a few at a go. When they are golden brown and crisp on one side, turn them over. Halfway through frying, you may have to wipe out the oil and start again with fresh oil and butter, as the loose breadcrumbs can start to burn quite easily. When evenly coloured, you can place them on a baking tray ready to finish cooking in the oven. Finish frying all the escalopes of pork. Season lightly, bake in the oven for about 10 minutes and then serve while still hot with lemon wedges. These are also tasty eaten cold, but I also reheated them in the oven for about 20 minutes the next day and even though they were a bit dried out, they were still delicious.

63

spiced pork skewers

2 tsp smoked sweet paprika
2 tsp fennel seeds
Good pinch dried chilli
1 tsp turmeric
1 tsp garam masala
1 tsp curry powder
$^{1}/_{2}$ tsp ground ginger
$^{1}/_{2}$ tsp cinnamon
Lots of salt and black pepper
Juice and zest of 1 lemon
2 cloves garlic, peeled
3 tbsp olive oil
650 g pork fillet, trimmed and diced into decent-sized chunks

This recipe is perfect for the Irish weather, which can be haphazard at the best of times. The pork skewers can be done on a barbecue if the weather's nice or in the oven or grill if the rain arrives. The yoghurt with a spoonful of good store-bought tomato chutney is also a brilliant instant condiment for this type of meat dish. Feel free to mix and match spices for the pork marinade and use the list below as a guideline only – a bit of tweaking won't matter.

Serves 4

Whizz all the spice ingredients together with the lemon juice, zest, garlic and olive oil. Put the pork in a shallow dish or bowl and spoon in the spice rub. Mix well and ensure the pork is well coated. Marinate overnight if you can or for a few hours at least. Then you can either roast in a hot oven (say 200°C for about 18 minutes) or under the grill until slightly charred and cooked through. Or you can barbecue the pork by threading it onto skewers and cooking till nicely charred on all sides and well cooked. Serve with a big dollop of the yoghurt and maybe a nice rice salad.

For the tomato yoghurt:
200 g Greek yoghurt
1–2 tbsp tomato chutney
Bunch coriander, finely chopped

Mix and taste. Season and chill until ready to serve. This sauce can actually woo children away from ketchup.

Recommended side: *Wild rice and sweetcorn salad (p. 294).*

roast pork with prune, pine nut and spinach stuffing

1 pork fillet

1 onion, peeled and diced

2 tbsp olive oil

4 smoked streaky rashers, diced

2 cloves garlic, peeled and crushed

Approx. 150 g baby spinach

130 g stoned prunes, chopped

2 tbsp pine nuts, toasted

Salt and pepper

4–6 slices Parma ham

Big knob butter

8–10 shallots, peeled

1 tbsp redcurrant jelly

This moreish pork dish is always a big favourite as it's very filling and full of salty flavour, yet has a hint of sweetness thanks to the redcurrant jelly. It's perfect for feeding a big family or a group of hungry friends.

Serves 4–6

Preheat the oven to 180°C. Slice the pork fillet in half lengthways, but not all the way through. Put between two sheets of cling film and bash with a rolling pin to turn it into one large rectangle of flattened pork fillet.

Sweat the onion in the olive oil till soft and then turn up the heat and add the rashers and fry till brown and crisp. Add the garlic, spinach, prunes and pine nuts and sauté till the spinach wilts. Keep the heat turned up so that any water from the spinach evaporates. Season and set aside to cool.

Once the stuffing is completely cold, you can stuff the pork and leave overnight, ready to cook. But if you are cooking it straightaway then it's alright to stuff the pork while the stuffing is still warm. Spoon the stuffing in a straight line right down the middle of the pork, then roll up and wrap the pork in the Parma ham. Tie at intervals with string and then roast in a roasting tray for about 20 minutes.

Meanwhile, heat up the butter and sweat the shallots in a saucepan until golden brown. Take the pork out of the oven, add the buttery shallots to the roasting tray and smear the pork with the redcurrant jelly. Baste with the juices, season with black pepper and roast for about another 20 minutes. So, cook the pork for 40 minutes in total. Leave to rest for 10 minutes before carving and serving with the shallots and pan juices.

Recommended side: *Balsamic potatoes (p. 274).*

roast loin of bacon with dried cherries and plums

1 kg loin of bacon

250 ml sherry

100 ml sherry vinegar

Zest of 1 lemon

4 tbsp olive oil

5 tbsp honey

1 tbsp brown sugar

3-inch piece ginger, peeled and very finely sliced

6 cloves garlic, peeled and very finely sliced

1 onion, peeled and chopped

160 g dried cranberries or cherries

4 plums, cut in half, stone removed

The glaze for this roast loin of bacon is a bit more exciting than the mustard and honey or brown sugar ones that tend to be the default setting. The loin used here weighs about 1 kg and so would be perfect for a slice for at least 6–8 guests.

Serves 6–8

Preheat the oven to 180°C. Put the loin of bacon into a deep roasting dish. In a bowl, mix all the other ingredients together to make the glaze. Score the bacon and then pour the glaze over, packing the chunkier bits on to the meat as much as possible. I bake it for an hour with the foil on for half the cooking time, then remove it for the second half so the sugar starts to caramelise.

Slice and serve with a good spoonful of the glaze and half a plum.

Recommended side: *Paprika and onion roast potato (p. 290).*

66

pork fillet with celeriac and onion purée

This roast pork gets that tricky balance right between winter richness and spring lightness. It is also easy enough to do, particularly if you do most of the prep work in advance.

Serves 4

You can reheat the celeriac purée, so it's best to do it first. The pork can be cooked by being browned first and then finished off in the oven, which will give you breathing space to reheat the purée and get your plates organized for dishing up.

So, starting with the celeriac purée: in a medium-sized saucepan, heat the milk with the celeriac chunks, thyme and 3 whole cloves of garlic. Put a lid on and bring up to a gentle simmer and cook for about 15 minutes or so until soft. Then allow to cool and put the celeriac and garlic in a blender, discard the thyme sprigs and keep the milk. While you are cooking the celeriac, sweat the onions in the olive oil with the lid on until very soft, usually about 20 minutes. Add them to the celeriac and season lightly.

Add a good ladleful of milk and blend, adding more milk until you have a nice, soft purée – not 'slop', but soft. So go easy with the milk at the start. You can do this the day before, as long as you let it cool down fully and then refrigerate. Just reheat with a knob of butter and a little more milk (either the reserved stuff or splash of new stuff) as the fridge tends to dry out these things. Check the seasoning and serve when you're ready.

Preheat the oven to 180°C. To cook the pork, heat the butter and good splash of olive oil in a large frying pan until foaming. Fry the fillets on a high heat, ensuring a good, high sizzle, season well and fry them until well coloured on all sides. Then deglaze the pan with the wine (be careful of flames) and add the chopped garlic and thyme. Spoon and baste the fillets in all the juices and transfer to a roasting tray. Roast in the oven for about 15 minutes. Heat up your purée, spoon the juices over the pork and then cover in foil and allow to rest for about 5 minutes, keeping them warm. Slice and arrange neatly on the plate, spoon over some more juices and serve.

400 ml whole milk

1 celeriac, peeled and cut into chunks

Few sprigs thyme

3 cloves garlic, peeled

2 large onions, peeled and finely sliced

3 tbsp olive oil

Salt and pepper

2 large pork fillets (approx. 400 g each), trimmed of all sinew and excess fat

50 g butter

Splash olive oil

Couple of glasses white wine

2 cloves garlic, peeled and roughly chopped

Few more sprigs thyme

67

aubergines stuffed with spiced pork

2–3 aubergines, each weighing 220 g approx.

Approx. 150 ml olive oil

Salt and pepper

100 g breadcrumbs

80 ml milk

1 small onion, peeled and chopped

250 g minced pork

2 cloves garlic, peeled and crushed

$1/2$ tsp ground cinnamon

$1/2$ tsp ground cumin

1 dessertspoon red wine vinegar or sherry vinegar

1 large tomato, roughly chopped

50 g Parmesan

1 egg, beaten

120 g cheddar, grated

Chopped parsley, to serve

Claudia Roden's book The Food of Spain *is a delightful read, with lots of dishes that taste great and are simple rather than exotic or fancy. For this dish, the idea of steaming the aubergines before stuffing them didn't appeal, so they were roasted instead and it worked out well. The filling is delightful with the addition of cinnamon, cumin and garlic and they make a perfect as a starter or main course. They are an all-round family hit.*

Serves 3–4

Preheat the oven to 180°C. Cut the aubergines in half and place on a baking tray or two. Score the flesh and drizzle generously with olive oil and season with salt and pepper. Bake for about 20 minutes. Let them cool and when easily handled, spoon out the flesh and leave it aside in a bowl.

Mix the breadcrumbs and milk together. Sweat the onion in a 2 large tablespoons of olive oil. Then add the aubergine pulp – chop this up a bit if it's not mushy enough – and the minced pork. Add the garlic and spices and cook for a few minutes. Season well, and then add the vinegar and tomato. Stir and continue to cook till the mixture gets quite dry and the juice from the tomato and vinegar disappears. The meat will cook fully, so don't worry about this. You are stuffing the aubergines with a fully cooked mixture. Remove from the heat and allow to cool for 5 minutes. Add the Parmesan and beaten egg. Mix well, then spoon into the hollow boats of aubergines. Sprinkle with the cheddar cheese another glug of olive oil, some salt and pepper and bake for about 25 minutes until golden brown and bubbling.

Let them cool down for about 10–15 minutes before serving. They are also good cold and they reheat well the next day at about 180°C for 15 minutes, although you may want to cover them loosely with foil so the cheese doesn't brown too much. A good sprinkle of parsley, some bread and a mixed green salad make this a wonderful supper.

sticky pork

Good splash olive oil

1 kg pork shoulder, cut into 2 cm chunks

1–2 tbsp honey

1 tbsp Chinese five-spice powder

1 tbsp Szechuan peppercorns

2 tbsp soy sauce

Approx. 500 ml water

Another squeeze of honey or maple syrup and soy sauce

3 cloves garlic, peeled and crushed

To serve:

Mixed leaves

Beansprouts

Radishes

Spring onions

Sprinkle of sesame seeds

This dish has the same bite and flavours as sweet and sticky spare ribs or pulled pork, but with less fat and less hassle. I use pork shoulder, which is cheap and tender as anything after an initial searing on the stove followed by an hour-long gentle braise in the oven. One final blast to reduce the flavoursome liquid in the saucepan and it's all done. You can serve it with some mixed leaves, sprouts, radishes and a sprinkle of sesame seeds, but it would also be delicious sitting on top of wild rice with some steamed broccoli or bok choy.

Serves 4–6

Preheat the oven to 170°C. Heat up the olive oil in a large frying pan that can go in the oven. If you don't have one that is ovenproof, you can just transfer the seared pork to a casserole dish.

Sear the pork in the very hot oil until starting to brown and char. If your pan isn't big enough, you may need to do this in 2 batches. When you're starting to get somewhere with the colour, add in the honey, which will move things along. Then add in the five-spice, the peppercorns and the soy sauce. After a few more minutes of cooking, things should be a nice dark brown colour. Carefully add in the water, which should deglaze the pan, and cover with foil.

Cook the pork in the oven for about an hour. Most of the water should remain and very little should have cooked off, but if you find all of it evaporating, keep the pork topped up with water. Then put back on the hob and simmer until the sauce reduces right down.

At this stage you should taste the pork and make sure it's quite tender and that it's tasty. It may need another squeeze of honey, some garlic and another splash of soy sauce. The heat will cook off any liquid and once you have a sticky, tasty dish, leave it to settle for a few minutes while you serve up your salad, rice or vegetables. Serve the pork with whatever garnish you fancy.

69

pork, fennel and olive stew

Olive oil

2 large onions, peeled and diced

4 fennel, sliced

Loads of rosemary

1 head garlic, peeled and roughly chopped

30 g tin anchovies in olive oil

Lemon juice and rind

2 kg boned pork shoulder, rind removed, cut into good chunks

1 heaped tbsp tomato purée

1 pinch cinnamon

1 bottle red wine

200 g wrinkly, stoned black olives

The pork and fennel stew came from Valentine Warner, who's got lots of brilliant recipes in his cookbooks. It is also quite handy in the sense that you don't have to brown the meat off first, which does speed up the whole process of getting it in the oven to cook. The cinnamon in this version has also been cut down considerably. You can serve it with polenta for a bit of variety, or with some straightforward boiled potatoes. Either way, it is a lovely dish, and the fat in the pork shoulder seems to melt down quite quickly.

Serves 8

Preheat oven to 170°C. In a large, heavy-based saucepan, for which you have a lid, heat up a good few glugs of olive oil and sweat the onions and fennel for about 10 minutes until very soft, with the lid on. Add the rosemary, garlic, anchovies, lemon juice and rind and season very well. When this base is really quite soft and wilted down, add the pork, the tomato purée and a pinch of cinnamon. Mix really well and then add in the red wine. Bring up to a simmer, then cover with a lid and put in the oven for at least 2 hours, stirring every 30 minutes or so.

After about 2 hours, check the consistency; you may want to remove the lid for the final 30 minutes of cooking, which is when you should chuck in the olives. Taste, season and reduce if necessary.

70

pork larb

1 tbsp olive or rapeseed oil

3-inch piece ginger, grated or diced

1 red chilli, very finely sliced

2 sticks lemongrass, thinly sliced

3 kaffir lime leaves, crushed

Approx. 600 g minced pork

2 tbsp fish sauce

Juice of 2 limes

1–2 heads baby gem or butter leaf lettuce

Bunch coriander

Few pistachios

Few mint leaves

Larb (or laab, plus a few other spellings) is the national dish of Laos and although many traditional versions use puffed or toasted rice, I've kept this recipe simple. You could argue that it's as inauthentic as you can get, but a big frying pan's worth of crumbled and well-seasoned meat doled out into leaves of butter lettuce always gets wolfed down. This recipe uses pork, but you could use minced chicken or turkey or even a selection of tough vegetables such as carrots, cabbage and sweet potato plus a few mushrooms at the end.

Serves 3–4

Heat up the oil in a large frying pan and sear the ginger, chilli, lemongrass and lime leaves to make a fragrant base in which to sauté the pork. After a minute or so, add the pork. Smash it up with a wooden spoon and move it around so that it breaks into smaller chunks and starts to separate rather than remain as one big mound. The idea is to lightly brown the pork and coat it evenly with the fragrant flavours.

After about five minutes, add the fish sauce. Keep the heat up and keep cooking until it starts to char a bit in places and is really cooked through. Then remove from the heat and allow to cool. Taste and adjust the seasoning.

Add some lime juice, which will sharpen up the flavour, then spoon into the lettuce leaves, top with chopped coriander, a few crushed pistachios and even a little mint. Serve up and watch them disappear. An extra wedge of lime is also nice to serve.

71

crisp ham hock with plum chutney

2 tbsp olive oil

1 onion, peeled and sliced

1 clove garlic, peeled and chopped

1 celery stick, chopped

1 carrot, peeled and chopped

Few sprigs thyme

2 bay leaves

A few whole black peppercorns

2 ham hocks

250 ml cider vinegar

2 tbsp honey

This German dish of roasted pork knuckle, or ham hock, is especially popular in Bavaria. It's usually served with heaps of cabbage and potatoes or some sort of dumpling, which is nice and delicious, but this is a more 'crispy' approach, served on toasted sourdough with a pungent chutney to cut through the rich, fatty, salty meat. Otherwise, you can just use the meat to go with a lovely lentil salad instead.

Serves 4–6

In a large saucepan that has a lid, heat up the olive oil and roughly sweat the onion, garlic, celery and carrot. Add the thyme and bay leaves. Add in a few peppercorns and then gently place the ham hocks in the saucepan – you don't need to do any prep to them at all. Then top up with enough water to cover the ham hocks, add the cider vinegar and bring up to simmer, occasionally skimming any scum that rises to the surface. Cook gently for at least 2 hours.

Once cooked, let the ham hocks settle and cool down in the water for about 30 minutes. Then gently fish them out and set aside until cool enough to handle. You can keep the stock as a delicious, salty base for a lovely soup, but be sure to strain it to get rid of the vegetable debris. You can reduce it down by half if fridge space is an issue.

Discard the really fatty bits of the ham hock, tear the meat into shards and then place it on a roasting tray and drizzle the honey over it. Grill it until really crisp. It is also delicious tossed through salads and can be used in many pasta dishes to give sublime flavour. It's also really nice with buttered toast, chutney and a crisp green salad.

quick plum chutney

125 ml cider vinegar

150 g caster sugar

3 plums, stoned and chopped

3-inch piece ginger, peeled and sliced

1 onion, peeled and very finely diced

Put all the ingredients together in a saucepan with a lid on and gently cook together until simmering and bubbling. Simmer for about 10 minutes. Taste and season, and chill down until ready to serve.

Recommended sides: *Winter salad (but leave out the chorizo and just use the crisp ham hock instead) (p. 304).*

72

potted pork with raisins and thyme

400 g minced pork

4 rashers streaky bacon, diced

1 clove garlic, peeled and crushed

Pinch mace

Bunch thyme (leaves from 8–10 sprigs)

100 g raisins

50 g shelled pistachios

8 juniper berries, crushed

1 tsp black peppercorns, crushed

Splash of brandy or sherry

1 tsp fennel seeds

If you are looking for something that is nice to eat while sitting around chatting with friends but which is not necessarily a full meal, savoury treats on large platters or boards work a dream. They're perfect when no one expects 'dinner', but just enough fodder to keep everyone nicely fed while they enjoy a glass of wine. This recipe, inspired by the inimitable Delia Smith, has a decidedly 1980s feels to it, which makes it positively on trend!

Serves 8

Preheat the oven to 150°C. Mix all the ingredients together and press into a bowl or terrine dish. Fill a deep roasting tin halfway up with boiling water to make a bain-marie, and place the terrine dish or bowl in the middle. Put the whole lot in the oven and cook for 2 hours. Cool down and serve cold on a platter with Melba toast, with rocket, apple balsamic and roasted sliced apple as a garnish.

FISH AND SHELLFISH

73

prawns with garlic and feta

100 g butter

8 cloves garlic, peeled and crushed

Good pinch chilli flakes

Splash olive oil

1 kg frozen prawns

Salt and pepper

Bunch flat-leaf parsley, finely chopped

Juice of 2 lemons

200 g feta cheese, finely diced

You can serve this dish either as individual prawns with some of the feta and garlic butter drizzled on top or put them on some bread for a kind of delicious prawns on toast dish. You can use whatever prawns are handy: frozen, cooked or uncooked.

Serves 10

You might need to do this in two batches, depending on the size of your frying pan. Either way, have a big platter or some bits of toast ready.

Melt half or all of the butter and add the garlic, chilli and a splash of olive oil. When hot (but don't let the garlic burn) add the prawns and turn up the heat. Cook them out, tossing regularly so they are well coated in butter and garlic. Season with plenty of black pepper and a little salt. Add the chopped parsley, the lemon juice and finally the feta. Mix well and when it's hot through and the prawns are fully cooked, spoon onto the platter or onto the toast. Eat immediately.

74

lemon sole parcels

4 small skinless fillets of lemon sole (or plaice)

Juice of 1 lemon

Big bunch flat-leaf parsley, finely chopped

1 tbsp capers

50 g flaked almonds

1–2 tbsp olive oil

Salt and pepper

This is fast food at its very best and is the kind of dish that doesn't even need a recipe; it's really just a question of throwing it all together. Flaked almonds are a great store-cupboard ingredient that gives a nice crunch to savoury dishes without taking over, unlike some nuts, and a big bunch of flat-leaf parsley works a treat to keep it green. Once you have skinned the fillets, this recipe takes just minutes to prepare and about 15 minutes in the oven. Simple, light and delicious.

Serves 2 (2 small fillets per person)

Preheat the oven to 180°C. In a medium-sized gratin dish, lightly oil the base and then lay down 2 fish fillets. Mix together the lemon juice, parsley, capers, almonds and olive oil. Season with pepper and mix so that it forms a really rough sort of salsa. Spoon this on top of each fish fillet and then top with the other fillet and press down. Season the outside of the fish and drizzle with some more olive oil.

Then bake, uncovered for 10–15 minutes, depending on the size of your fillets and how cold your ingredients were to begin with. Let them rest for a minute before transferring onto a plate. Some boiled potatoes or purple sprouting broccoli would be lovely with this.

Recommended side: *Garlic roasted new potato salad (p. 288).*

75

Korean salmon

400 g salmon fillets, skin removed

4 tbsp light sesame oil

50 ml soy sauce

4 cloves garlic, peeled and finely chopped

Good pinch chilli flakes

Black pepper

1 tbsp black or white sesame seeds

2 tbsp sweet chilli sauce

This is a beautifully simple and tasty dish that will make you feel healthy after eating it. It's light and spicy and is perfectly accompanied by chopped spring onions, sharp green salad and a glass of chilled white wine. If you want to avoid the refined sugar in the chilli sauce, then you can always use a little squeeze on honey and some chilli flakes instead.

Serves 2

Cut the salmon into big chunks – or you can leave whole. You'll have enough marinade to do a third 200 g fillet, but if you want to serve more fish, just double the marinade quantities. Mix all the other ingredients together and marinate the fish for a few hours or overnight. Cook on a wire rack, under a hot grill until charred and cooked through. You can baste with extra marinade while cooking. Serve with some chopped spring onions and a salad.

Recommended side: *Asparagus with miso butter (p. 246).*

76

kedgeree light

1 tbsp olive oil

2 bunches spring onions, chopped

1 good tbsp mild curry powder

150 g mushrooms, finely sliced

300 g brown basmati rice

Approx. 600 ml vegetable stock

100 g frozen peas

4 eggs

To garnish:

Smoked mackerel, trout or salmon

Chopped cherry tomatoes

Handful pistachio nuts

Bunch coriander or parsley

This kedgeree comes from Fresh Energy Cookbook *by raw food guru Natalia Rose and chef Doris Choi (also my sister-in-law). It's a great book full of interesting nutritional tips about detoxing, food combining and making the body less acidic, all of which to help promote a better, healthier lifestyle. Even children will enjoy this dish and it will definitely fit into a midweek supper repertoire. It takes less than 45 minutes from start to table. You can use either boiled eggs for this or just let raw eggs cook when you're heating it up.*

Serves 4

Have the mushrooms ready to go in as they will add some moisture to the pan. Heat the olive oil in a heavy-based saucepan and sweat the spring onions with the curry powder. Mix well, but be careful as it can burn. Add the prepared mushrooms. Then add in the rice. Mix well so the grains are coated, and then add in the stock. Put a tight-fitting lid on and cook for about 30 minutes over a gentle heat.

Then remove the lid; practically all of the water should be gone. Check you have no burnt patches, chuck in the peas and put the lid back on and leave it to sit and steam.

At this stage, it is ready to go. You can add in the eggs and stir around. The heat will cook them but if you feel it's cooled down too much, you can heat it up for another minute or so. If it's too dry, add a good splash of water from a boiled kettle. Serve with chopped coriander or parsley, nuts and bits of smoked fish, cherry tomatoes or even some avocado.

77

herb-and-curry-crusted fish fillets

400 g white fish fillets

Good glug olive oil

Salt and pepper

Approx. 2–3 dessertspoons of mayonnaise

1 clove garlic, peeled and crushed

1 tsp mild curry powder

Zest and juice of 1 lemon

100 g breadcrumbs

Bunch flat-leaf parsley or coriander

Kids will love these herb-and-curry-crusted fish fillets and although you can ditch the curry powder, a lot of them actually like it. It's good to expand the taste buds in this way but please tweak to suit your own household. The lemon in the breadcrumbs gives it a good kick, but again, some people may find this overpowering. It's a straightforward dish that is user-friendly and will be a bit of a crowd pleaser. Not dinner-party nosh, but perfect for when you really have 30 minutes to get dinner on the table.

Serves 4

Preheat the oven to 200°C. Place the fish in a shallow gratin dish and drizzle with olive oil and season lightly. Mix together the mayonnaise, garlic, curry powder and lemon juice. Spread a layer over each piece of the fish. Mix the breadcrumbs with the lemon zest, salt and pepper and the parsley or coriander. This is easier to do in a food processor but if you don't have one or you're too lazy to wash it up, just chop the herbs like crazy and give it a good mix with the breadcrumbs. Add a couple of glugs of olive oil to the crumbs. Sprinkle this generously over the mayonnaise topping and then bake for about 15 minutes. The fish should be well cooked through and the crumbs should just be starting to brown in parts. Serve with a big salad and if you need starch to go with it, some boiled rice will do.

Recommended side: *Roast parsnips and carrots with fennel, honey and seeds (p. 258).*

grilled mackerel with beetroot, orange and olive salsa

4 raw beetroots

1 orange, peeled and segmented

100 g stoned kalamata olives, roughly chopped

2 spring onions, finely sliced

Big bunch parsley, chopped

Big bunch basil, chopped

Olive oil

Pinch chilli flakes

Salt and pepper

1 tbsp harissa paste

Large knob butter

4 mackerel fillets

Another homage to the great Ottolenghi – I made a few changes to the salsa, but love his suggestion of making the harissa butter. This salsa would be lovely with any kind of fish or even some grilled chicken, but the mackerel really stands up well to it, as oily fish can take a lot of citrus flavours.

Serves 4

Preheat the oven to 160°C. To make the salsa, roast the beetroot in tinfoil till tender – about 45 minutes – and then peel and dice. Then, in a bowl, toss the diced beetroot with the orange segments, olives, spring onions, chopped herbs and a slick of olive oil. Add some chilli if you like it hot and season. Set aside and keep at room temperature.

Next, heat your grill till it's super hot. Mix the harissa paste into the butter. Score the skin on the mackerel (this will stop it curling up), dot the harissa butter onto the fillets and grill skin-side up until crisp – about 7 minutes or so. Be careful not to burn them, though a little charring is okay. You don't need to cook them on both sides, but you can if you like your fish really well done. Serve with lots of salsa.

79

super-healthy salmon and tuna fishcakes

1 piece lemongrass

2 red onions, peeled and diced

2 lime leaves

2 red chillies, deseeded and diced

Small bunch coriander

Small bunch basil

2-inch piece ginger, peeled

2 tbsp tamari (or regular soy sauce)

1 tsp fish sauce

Splash sesame oil

Juice of 2 limes

200 g fresh salmon fillet, skin removed, roughly chopped

200 g fresh tuna fillet, skin removed, roughly chopped

Handful sesame seeds

These healthy fishcakes are dairy-free, wheat-free and low fat – and very tasty. Also, if you use tamari sauce instead of soy, they are perfect for coeliacs.

Serves 4 as a starter, 2 as a main

Preheat the oven to 200°C. Whizz all the ingredients – apart from the fish – together in the food processor until smooth. Add the fish and pulse so that it's processed, but not mushy or like baby food in texture. Have a baking tray ready with a sheet of greaseproof paper. Shape the fish into balls and place on the tray. If you can, chill for 10 minutes. Sprinkle with sesame seeds and then bake on a high heat for 10–12 minutes. If you can, gently turn them over halfway through, so they can brown on both sides. They do cook quite quickly, and you may like to serve them a bit rare inside. Let them settle for a second before removing from the paper (they are quite delicate as there is no egg to bind them) and then serve with this home-made chilli sauce.

Sweet chilli sauce

200 ml water

1 chilli with seeds in it

1 red pepper, with seeds, just the stalk removed

50 g sugar

50 ml white wine vinegar

2-inch piece ginger, peeled

1 stick lemongrass

Few lime leaves

2 cloves garlic

Salt

Stalks off a bunch of coriander – save the leaves for later

There is a lot of sugar in this, but a lot less than commercial varieties. Store in a jar in your fridge.

Put everything in a pot and bring to the boil. Let it simmer gently for about 45 minutes until jammy in texture and then remove from the heat and blend until smooth. Once cool, add in the chopped coriander leaves.

80

fish fingers

500 g skinless salmon fillet

Approx. 75 g breadcrumbs (brown bread is good)

1 tbsp Parmesan, finely grated

Lemon zest (optional)

Fresh herbs, chopped (optional)

Black pepper (optional)

1 egg, beaten

1–2 tsp olive oil

It is nice to prepare dishes that remind us of our youth, but which we can now recreate into healthier versions for ourselves and our families. For example, these fish fingers come from The Food Hospital, *a cookbook devoted to recipes designed to improve most ailments with good nutrition. They are much better for you than any shop-bought ones – and much tastier. These would be lovely served with peas and broccoli.*

Serves 4

Preheat the oven to 200°C. If your fishmonger is a friendly type of person, ask them to cut the fillets into finger-sized thick strips, though you can just do it yourself. I cheat and use white breadcrumbs, but do use brown bread ones – they're nicer and better for you. Mix the breadcrumbs with some Parmesan. If you want to broaden out the flavours, this is a good way to smuggle in some lemon rind, herbs or even a little black pepper. Dip the salmon into the egg and then the breadcrumbs. Lightly coat and then place on a baking tray that you should lightly oil with the olive oil. Bake for about 12 minutes. Maybe turn them over after ten minutes and leave them on for a few more minutes until nice and crisp on all sides. Once they're crisp, they're cooked.

baked fish 'pie'

2–3 large baking potatoes

Approx. 100 g diced fish
(salmon, haddock, coley, cod)

100 ml milk

Good knob butter

Salt and pepper

Bay leaf or grate of nutmeg
(optional)

Garlic or mild curry powder
(optional)

100 g frozen peas

1 Savoy cabbage, very finely
sliced

50 g grated cheddar

The baked spuds in this recipe help to bulk up this short-cut fish pie and saves you the bother of preparing a béchamel sauce and making too much effort, but still gets some fish and greens in. You may even find a frozen fish mix in the supermarket, which is a handy way to be able to dump some fish into a saucepan and get supper on the table in a hurry. The potatoes for this are baked the day before so they can be made in a flash on the night. Feel free to leave out the cabbage and just use peas. This isn't the most gourmet recipe in the world, but it's easy and good for reluctant fish-eaters.

Preheat the oven to 200°C. Make a slit around the potatoes and bake for about 40–50 minutes until tender inside – stick a knife into them to check. You could bake these a day or two in advance. If so, don't bother scooping them out, just take them out of the fridge, and then when you are ready to make the dish, scoop out the cold flesh and start as per below.

Get the fish mix ready about 15 minutes before you are finished baking the spuds. In a small saucepan, heat up the fish along with the milk and knob of butter. You can season this lightly or even add a bay leaf or little scrape of nutmeg. Feel free to introduce some garlic or even a small pinch of mild curry powder. Once you have won over the children with these potatoes, you can start manipulating the flavours to help them to develop interest in new flavours.

The fish will cook very quickly. Just leave it on a gentle heat to simmer for a few minutes and when the pieces start to look a little opaque, add the peas. Remove from the heat after another minute or so and let sit. It will keep cooking while you scoop out the potato flesh into a bowl.

Blanch the cabbage and drain. Take half – or even a quarter – and add it to the spuds. (The rest of the cabbage you can eat all by itself with a little knob of butter or splash of tamari soy sauce.)

Mix everything well and taste. You may want to add a spoonful of yoghurt if you feel they are a bit dry. Then spoon back into the spuds, top with cheese and bake for about 10 minutes at 200°C. You can also brown them under a grill before serving.

82

seared scallops with sweet chilli sauce and crème fraîche

For the sweet chilli sauce:
150 g caster sugar
10 cloves garlic, peeled
4 red chillies
1/2 whole hand of ginger, peeled and roughly chopped
8 lime leaves
3 lemongrass stems, roughly chopped
Big bunch coriander
100 ml cider vinegar
3 tbsp fish sauce
3 tbsp soy sauce

For the scallops:
3–5 scallops per person
Olive oil or big knob butter
Salt and pepper
Bunch rocket
300 g crème fraîche
Squeeze lime juice

The delicious sweet chilli sauce comes from New Zealand chef and fusion innovator Peter Gordon and it would be just as tasty with fish such as monkfish, salmon or even with grilled chicken. It could also be used as a perfect dunking sauce for chargrilled prawns.

Put 200 ml water in a heavy-based saucepan and add the sugar. Don't stir; just heat it up until the sugar dissolves and then turn up the heat and gently simmer until the sugar turns a nice caramel colour. Meanwhile, whizz all the other ingredients together until they form a slightly chunky paste. You don't want it as smooth as soup, but you do need to make light work of the hunks of ginger, garlic and lemongrass. Take the caramel off the heat, carefully add the paste and whisk gently. Put back on the heat for a few minutes as this will help all those flavours to open up. Allow to cool and drizzle over the scallops. A little goes a long way.

To finish, sear the scallops in hot oil or butter for a minute or two on each side. Season lightly and then place on top of some rocket. Season the crème fraîche with the lime juice, salt and pepper and drizzle on top of the scallops, along with a few blobs of the sweet chilli sauce.

83

scallop ceviche

¹/₂ cucumber, deseeded, peeled and very finely diced

¹/₂ red onion, peeled and diced

1 small chilli, deseeded and diced

Juice of 2 limes

Salt and pepper

300 g scallops

Bunch coriander, very finely chopped

Splash olive oil

This scallop ceviche dish is a good example of a 'no-cook' dish that is lovely served in small shot glasses. It can be kept chilling nicely and then brought out to enjoy as a starter that guests can eat while standing. Any good raw fish can be substituted for the scallops – salmon, monkfish and sea bass work nicely when cold-cooked.

Serves 6–8 in shot glasses

Mix together the cucumber, red onion, chilli and lime juice and season very well. Remove the little muscle that is attached to the roe of the scallops and discard it along with the roe. (If you do like the roe, you can stick it in the freezer to use in a seafood pasta sauce, fish pie or pâté.) Very finely slice or dice the scallops and mix with the rest of the ingredients. Chill down and marinate for about 30 minutes. This is fine for a few hours in the fridge but will probably need more salt, as it will taste blander cold than at room temperature. Serve in chilled glasses.

84

zingy crab cakes

500 g cooked crab, drained

1 green chilli, deseeded and very finely sliced

4 spring onions, very finely sliced

Zest and juice of 2 limes

Big bunch (approx. 20 g) flat-leaf parsley, chopped

Big bunch (approx. 20 g) coriander, chopped

Salt and pepper

Handful or two cream flour

1–2 eggs, beaten

Approx. 150 g panko or breadcrumbs

Sunflower oil

For the cocktail sauce:

150 g mayonnaise

2 tbsp ketchup

1 tbsp horseradish sauce

1 tbsp tomato purée

2 limes

Good pinch cayenne pepper

Salt and pepper

Few shakes Tabasco sauce

This is a nice summery dish, as the sauce is light and runny. You can buy packets of panko (Japanese breadcrumbs) in supermarkets these days, not just Asian stores or delis, but if you can't find them, regular breadcrumbs will do.

Serves 4 (or 8 as a starter)

Really drain the crabmeat to get as much liquid out of it as possible. Mix with the chilli, spring onions, lime zest and juice, parsley and coriander and season with a little salt and plenty of black pepper. Roughly divide into 8 and then shape into patties. They will feel very wet, so spread out the flour on a plate and just give them a little dusting with it. Then give them a light dunk in the beaten egg, and then a last coating in the panko or breadcrumbs. Lay them out on a tray or large plate and refrigerate for an hour or so if you can. Cover loosely with foil. The fridge will cool them down and also dry them out a bit, making them easier to fry.

When you are ready to cook, heat up some sunflower oil in a large non-stick frying pan and fry them carefully on each side for a few minutes until golden brown. Make sure the oil is hot enough and also that a nice golden brown coating forms before you try to turn them over. You may need to do this in two or three batches. (You can always keep them warm in the oven while you finish off the second batch.) Drain on kitchen paper and serve with the cocktail sauce.

To make the cocktail sauce, mix all the ingredients together, season well and chill until ready to serve.

Recommended side: *Wild rice and sweetcorn salad (p. 294).*

85

mussels with tomato, fennel and garlic

200 ml olive oil

6 cloves garlic

3 tsp fennel seeds

1–2 fennel bulbs, very finely diced

1 onion, peeled and sliced

8 tomatoes, roughly diced

4–6 slices sourdough, toasted

Salt and pepper

1 kg mussels, scrubbed and prepared (see above)

150 ml red wine

One of the nicest ways to cook mussels is to steam them with something thick, such as some cooking liquid emulsified with butter, a little white wine, sautéed shallot, lots of parsley, herbed breadcrumbs and garlic. This tomato sauce with lots of olive oil, fennel and garlic also works a treat, with garlic-rubbed bread in the bottom.

Do remember the basics about mussels: throw any open ones away; remove any barnacle-type bits with a small sharp knife; pull away any beards with your fingers; give them a good rinse; and discard any ones that are open or have broken or cracked shells. When you cook them, the shells will open up – then remember to throw away the ones that don't.

I would happily have this along side the tomato barley risotto, as long as I could scoop out all the mussels and spoon them – along with the sauce – over the barley, making it a kind of healthy mussel risotto!

Serves 4–6 as a starter

Heat the olive oil and 4 cloves of the garlic and cook for a minute. Add the fennel seeds, diced fennel and onion and cook very gently until really soft.

Meanwhile, toast the sourdough thoroughly and leave in the toaster or on a wire rack to cool so it doesn't go soggy. Then, using the last 2 cloves of garlic, cut them in half and rub the cut ends on the cool toast, almost as though you were grating the garlic clove along the crisp toast. This will create fantastic, garlic-flavoured pieces of sourdough.

Chuck the bits of garlic into the saucepan along with the fennel. Cut the bread into triangles and put in the bottom of 4–6 bowls. Add the tomatoes to the saucepan, stir and season. Cook with a lid on for about 5 minutes to let the tomatoes break down a bit.

Turn the heat up and then add the mussels and wine. Cover and cook for about 2–3 minutes. Give the pan a good shake every now and then. Take a look – provided you have good heat, hopefully most of the shells will now be open. Discard any that haven't opened.

Taste the tomato mix, season as needed and then spoon on top of the bread in each bowl and serve straight away, topped with lots of mussels.

Recommended side: *Tomato barley risotto (p. 286).*

86

grilled spiced fish skewers

2 cloves garlic, peeled and crushed

Juice of 1 lemon

Pinch chilli flakes

Good glug olive oil (approx. 50 ml)

Salt and pepper

$^1/_2$ tsp ground coriander

$^1/_2$ tsp ground cumin

1 tsp turmeric

Big bunch flat-leaf parsley, very finely chopped

1 kg firm white fish, skin removed, cut into chunks

You can do these fish skewers with lovely, firm chunks of white fish, which is obviously ideal, or, as I do, with sad little bits of supermarket fish. If you go the supermarket fish route, they will slide off the skewers, so feel free to forget the skewers and simply grill on a high heat until slightly charred in places and piping hot. Then put it all on one big plate and dig in. Any kind of couscous goes superbly with this recipe, but the jewelled one is especially good with it.

Serves 4–6

In a large bowl, mix the garlic with the lemon juice, chilli flakes, olive oil, salt, pepper, spices and parsley. Then add the fish chunks and stir gently so that the spices coat the fish. Set aside until ready to cook.

Thread the fish onto pre-soaked wooden skewers or metal skewers and cook under a hot grill on a wire rack until slightly charred and nice and hot. If you can, turn them over, though you may find the fish falls apart as it sticks to some of the bars of the wire rack. Let them settle for a minute before removing them and placing them on top of the couscous and serving.

Recommended side: *Jewelled couscous (p. 299).*

87

smoked haddock and spinach gratin

600 g fish chunks
2 bay leaves
Squeeze lemon juice
Black pepper
250 ml cream
100 g Parmesan, grated
1 tbsp wholegrain mustard
Few grates nutmeg
500 g baby spinach or approx. 450 g frozen leaf spinach, defrosted

Good knob butter
50 g breadcrumbs
Another large knob butter

This recipe comes from Lucas Hollweg's book Good Things to Eat, which is full of novel twists on old favourites. The recipe for the haddock gratin calls for 500 g of baby spinach that gets wilted down. This is fine, but frozen spinach is perfect for this kind of thing, as long as you thaw it out and squeeze it. I find the best way to do this is simply to leave it in the fridge overnight, then take it out of its pack, wrap it up in a really clean tea towel and squeeze like mad. This kind of gratin dish can be ruined by any sort of excess liquid swirling around the fish and turning a tasty topping into some sort of drenched, savoury sponge. You can use a combination of smoked haddock and some other chunks of white fish, but to be honest, it doesn't really matter. Trust your fishmonger to do the right thing.

Serves 4

Preheat the oven to 180°C. If you are using all smoked haddock, then put the fish in a small saucepan and just cover with some boiling water, the bay leaves, some pepper and lemon. Leave to cook very lightly. If you are using other fish, you probably don't need to do this. (This light 'bath' just helps get rid of excess smokiness.) Drain the fish and set aside.

Meanwhile, heat the cream, bay leaves and lemon juice on the stove and heat until simmering. Keep an eye on it but reduce by a third. Stir in the Parmesan and mustard, plus a few flecks of ground nutmeg and set aside. Sauté the spinach with a knob of butter and, if using fresh spinach, a few flecks of water. Then drain and squeeze dry and spread out into a gratin dish. Put the fish on top and pour over the reduced cream mixture. Sprinkle the breadcrumbs on top and then dot with the butter. Bake for 35 minutes until golden brown.

Recommended side: *Leek and bread pudding (p. 298).*

monkfish, lemongrass and coconut curry

2 onions, peeled and sliced

Few glugs olive oil

1 tbsp mild curry powder

3 cloves garlic, peeled and crushed

3-inch piece ginger, peeled and very finely sliced

½ chilli, deseeded and sliced (optional)

1–2 lemongrass, finely sliced

Salt and pepper

250 g new potatoes (approx. 6–8 spuds)

500 ml water or vegetable stock

400 ml coconut milk

3 star anise

3–4 dried lime leaves

50 g desiccated coconut

Approx. 1 kg diced monkfish

2 limes

Fish sauce (optional)

Bunch coriander, finely chopped

This kind of one-pot wonder is easy to make and can be bumped up to feed 12 or 18. It also works well with chicken or prawns, or with the monkfish as in the recipe below. You could even stay vegetarian by using hunks of courgette and aubergine in place of the fish. All you need are a big pot of rice and a few salads, and hey presto, lunch for the masses is sorted. Monkfish can be pricey so flesh this out with other firm white fish. Just be sure to ask your fishmonger to give you big chunks of firm and meaty fish that can go into a curry.

Serves 6–8

In a large heavy-based saucepan, sauté the onions in the olive oil for a few minutes until they're starting to soften down a bit. Keep moving them around so that they don't burn. Then sprinkle the curry powder on top and add in the garlic, ginger, chilli and lemongrass. Mix this around and season. It should start to smell really great after a few minutes. If you feel it's going to start burning in patches, add a splash of water to deglaze the pan, which will allow you to keep cooking it out.

Cut the potatoes in half or quarters, add them to the pot and get them well coated. Season again and then add in the stock and coconut milk. If you use water, you'll just have to season it more. Add the star anise, lime leaves and desiccated coconut. Simmer gently for about 20 minutes until the potatoes are getting tender.

You need to add the fish about 10 minutes before you want to serve, so if you're not ready to go to the table at this stage, you can leave the curry to cool down fully and then reheat, adding the fish to cook for about 10 minutes. It should be gently bubbling and simmering, so the fish will cook quickly, but you will need to taste and adjust the seasoning. If you feel it's a bit bland, some lime juice, fish sauce or salt will help. Serve with rice and some wedges of lime and chopped coriander.

89

curried mussels

2 knobs butter

1 onion, peeled and sliced

1 clove garlic, peeled and chopped

1 bay leaf

Pinch saffron (optional)

1 tbsp mild curry powder

1 kg mussels

125 ml white wine

100 g crème fraîche

Squeeze lemon juice

Bunch parsley, chopped

These curried mussels are so easy to prepare and should encourage us to cook them more often as they are a good source of selenium and B12, as well as folate and zinc. They are also cheap and plentiful, so you will be staying on the right side of sustainability. I rarely want to eat anything else with mussels except some hunks of sourdough bread, the ideal vehicle for sopping up all those lovely juices, accompanied by a nice green salad.

Serves 2 as a main course

In a heavy-based saucepan, sweat together the butter, onion, garlic, bay leaf and saffron (if using) with the lid on. When the onion is soft and translucent, add the curry powder and cook over a higher heat until you get a good whiff.

Add the mussels (see tip below) and then add in the wine. Cover and cook for 5 minutes. Lift the lid and check to see they are cooked and that they are all open. Discard any that aren't open.

Then spoon the mussels only into deep serving bowls (keep the juices in the pan) and set aside. Turn up the heat, and add the crème fraîche and lemon juice to the saucepan. Let it bubble and have a taste. Then adjust the seasoning, adding more garlic, lemon or a splash of wine if needed.

Pour the hot sauce over the warm mussels, garnish with parsley and serve.

TIP: *clean the mussels by giving them a good scrub and carefully removing any 'beards'. They should all be closed. Any that are wide open, throw out, but if they are open a bit, tap them closed and have a look. You'll actually see them closing slowly if you look carefully, and they should stay closed. If nothing is happening, and they're not closing, toss. When cooked, the shells will be open. Throw out any that aren't.*

barley and almond salad with spiced prawns

200 g pearl barley

1 cinnamon stick

Juice of 2 lemons

Juice of 1 lime

100 ml olive oil

2 tsp ground cumin

Salt and pepper

Large bunch coriander, finely chopped

Large bunch flat-leaf parsley, finely chopped

1 red onion, peeled and finely diced

1 head celery, finely chopped

500 g frozen prawns, defrosted and draining

Good knob butter

1 tbsp sumac or za'atar

2 cloves garlic

Sprinkle dried chilli flakes

Approx. 125 g mâche (lamb's lettuce)

Approx. 120 g flaked almonds, lightly toasted

This prawn and barley salad is perfect in warmer weather, when the chance of having a meal outside is starting to look like a possibility. You could also happily ditch the prawns and exchange them for some fried chunks of halloumi, which you can just chop into slices and fry in a little olive oil and a tiny bit of butter until golden brown. If time is of the essence, some hunks of feta will do.

Serves 4–6

Cook the pearl barley and cinnamon stick in boiling water until tender (about 25–30 minutes). Drain really well (discard the cinnamon stick) and then mix in a bowl with half of the lemon juice, all of the lime juice, half of the olive oil, all of the cumin and plenty of salt and pepper. Allow to cool and then mix with the coriander, parsley, red onion and celery. Set aside.

Heat up the rest of the olive oil in a large frying pan and throw in the prawns. Inevitably they will go a bit rubbery, but keep the heat up high and eventually the water in them will evaporate. Then add in the butter, sumac or za'atar, garlic and chilli. If you still feel not enough heat is happening, add in a sprinkle of sugar or squeeze of honey. This will get things colouring nicely. Season and then add the rest of the lemon juice, the garlic and the chilli.

When you are happy that the prawns are tasty, add the salad and mix together. Arrange the lettuce on a big plate, spoon the barley and prawns on top, scatter with toasted almonds and serve.

91

fishcakes in piquant tomato sauce

Big bunch parsley

Big bunch coriander

Big bunch chives

2 eggs

1 onion, peeled and diced

4 garlic cloves, peeled and crushed

100 g breadcrumbs

600 white fish, skinned and diced into 1 cm cubes (I use pollock, cod and hake)

For the sauce:

2 tbsp olive oil

1 onion, peeled and finely chopped

2 tsp sweet paprika

1 tsp ground coriander

Salt and pepper

125 ml white wine

2 chillies, finely chopped

400 g tinned chopped tomatoes

Pinch caster sugar

2 tbsp fish sauce

Mint leaves, finely chopped, to garnish

OK, Mr Ottolenghi: I promise I am not stalking you, but I love adapting your dishes. For this one, I ditched the pre-frying step, and I 'beefed up' the tomato sauce by using some fish sauce. You end up with a really healthy dish with a nice zingy feel to it. It is delicious with a green salad or some steamed greens and you will feel very virtuous after it.

Makes 12 patties

Preheat the oven to 180°C. First get the tomato sauce on the go: heat the olive oil and, over a medium heat, sweat the onion and spices until the onion is very soft. Season lightly with salt (remember, fish sauce is mega salty) and plenty of black pepper.

Add the wine and chillies and reduce the sauce to let the alcohol evaporate. Then add the tomatoes, a pinch of sugar and, finally, the fish sauce. Simmer gently for about 20 minutes and taste. Let it rest while you make the fishcakes.

For the fishcakes, start by blitzing the herbs with the eggs, onion and garlic in a food processor. Empty this mix into a bowl with the diced fish and shape the mixture into 12 roundish patties, about 6 cm across.

To cook the fishcakes, pour the tomato sauce into a casserole dish so it covers the bottom. Place the fishcakes on top and bake for about 30 minutes. To serve, garnish with some chopped mint.

92

baked sea trout

3 tsp cumin seeds

1 tsp coriander seeds

2 tsp caraway seeds

1 tsp smoked sweet paprika

Good pinch chilli flakes

3-inch piece ginger, peeled and roughly chopped

2 cloves garlic, peeled and roughly chopped

Zest and juice of 1 lemon

Good pinch salt

3 tbsp olive oil

1 whole sea trout (approx. 1.6 kg)

Baked trout is always a lovely thing to eat and the marinade here really complements it. The dish, which comes from the Modern Pantry, a quirky and trendy London restaurant, is wonderful to serve as part of a table full of food for friends and family to dig into.

Serves 4

Dry-roast the seeds in a frying pan for a minute or until you can get a good smell from them. Then put in a blender with all the ingredients (except for the sea trout) and blitz to make a rub. Make 3–4 slits in the fish diagonally on both sides and then place in a dish large enough to hold it. Slather the fish in the rub, inside and out, and leave for 30 minutes.

You can barbecue, grill or cook this in the oven at about 180°C for 20 minutes. Gently cut and pull away the top half and serve it onto a plate. Then pull up the main bone inside and serve up the bottom side of the fish.

Recommended side: *Lavash (p. 283), Jewelled couscous (p. 299) or Quinoa salad (p. 270).*

93

salmon and smoked haddock fishcakes

3 Desiree potatoes
(approx. 300 g)

400 ml milk

250 g smoked haddock

500 g salmon fillet, skinless

1 bunch spring onions, finely
chopped

Big bunch dill (approx. 25 g),
finely chopped

1 egg
Salt and pepper

For the coating:
1 egg, beaten
50 g plain flour
60 g breadcrumbs
Sunflower oil

These very plain fishcakes are based on an Adam Byatt recipe and are incredibly tasty. I've adapted it so you can fry them after crumbing or simply bake them with no crumb. Obviously, the breadcrumb-coated and fried ones taste better, but if you're being good, try the other method. As some people are not keen on smoked fish, feel free to make them all salmon if you prefer.

Serves 4–6 (about 12 fishcakes)

First, peel the spuds, then chop into bite-sized chunks and boil in salted water until tender. Drain, and then put back in the dry saucepan on a very low heat for a minute or so; put a tea towel on top to help dry them out. Be careful the tea towel does not go on fire! Mash the spuds up with a fork.

Meanwhile, heat up the milk slightly and when warm, carefully add the smoked haddock. Then bring up to a simmer. Add the salmon, bring back up to a simmer and then remove from the heat and set aside.

Drain the fish and remove any skin or bones and then transfer to a bowl and start to break it up and mash with a fork. Add the spring onions, dill and dried out spuds. Mix well, taste and season. Bind with the egg then shape into about 12 'burgers' and leave to cool down. At this stage you could refrigerate overnight (once they've cooled down to room temperature), covered with cling film, or keep going with the recipe.

If baking the fishcakes, preheat the oven to 200°C and put an empty baking tray in the oven to heat. Then get three plates or shallow bowls ready: one for the beaten egg, one for the flour and one for the breadcrumbs. Heat up the sunflower oil in a large frying pan. Dip the fishcakes in egg, flour and then breadcrumbs, and when the oil is hot, fry them in batches. Make sure they get a good golden brown crust on one side before you turn them over. Do this carefully, but with purpose, so they don't fall apart. When you have good colour on both sides, transfer all of them at the same time to the baking tray and finish cooking in the oven for about 10 minutes.

If you don't want to coat them in breadcrumbs or flour, then place the fishcakes onto a preheated baking tray and bake in the oven at 200°C for about 10 minutes. Then gently turn them over so that both sides get a chance to brown. Serve with the herb and garlic mayo.

garlic and herb mayo

2 egg yolks

1 whopping tbsp Dijon mustard

200 ml olive oil

200 ml sunflower oil

Juice of 1 lemon

Splash tarragon vinegar

3 cloves garlic, peeled and crushed

Handful dill, chopped

1 tsp pink peppercorns, crushed

Salt and pepper

Make sure the egg yolks are at room temperature. With a whisk, mix the egg yolks and mustard. Very slowly add a dribble of oil intermittently until you feel it thickening. Once this starts, you can be a bit more relaxed at the pace of adding the oils. Add about 3/4 of the oils, then mix in the seasonings: lemon juice, a splash of vinegar, garlic, dill, crushed peppercorns and salt. Mix well and then continue adding the oil until you have the right consistency. Chill until ready to serve.

Tip: *If you couldn't be bothered, then simply mix the mustard, dill, lemon juice and pink peppercorns into about 500 ml of store-bought mayo.*

Recommended side: *Summer crunchy caprese (p. 290).*

94

courgette, goat's cheese and mint frittata

4 courgettes, grated

100 ml olive oil

2 red onions, peeled and diced

Grate nutmeg

1 good tsp dried mint

8–10 eggs, beaten

Zest of 1 lemon

Salt and pepper

200 g soft goat's cheese

This courgette and mint frittata, which is good, wholesome grub, takes simple ingredients and makes them tastier and a lot more interesting to eat. You will need a large, ovenproof frying pan for this, preferably non-stick.

Serves 6 for light supper or lunch

Preheat the oven to 180°C. Put the grated courgettes in a sieve or colander, season with some salt and let them drain. Meanwhile, heat up half the olive oil and sweat the onions very gently. Then remove from the heat, add in the nutmeg and mint and set aside.

Press the courgettes down in the sieve to extract as much water as possible out of them and then scatter them around the saucepan. Add the lemon zest and then sprinkle the goat's cheese on top. Pour in the beaten eggs. You may want to loosen any clumps of courgettes or goat's cheese so that they are evenly dispersed.

Drizzle with the remaining olive oil and then bake for 25–30 minutes until pretty set. You can also give it a little go under the grill to give it a nice colour. Leave it to rest and then slice and serve with lovely crisp green salad.

95

mushroom and quinoa risotto

250 g quinoa

1 tbsp olive oil

30 g butter

1 onion, peeled and finely chopped

Salt and pepper

125 g button mushrooms, sliced

3 cloves garlic, peeled and sliced

250 ml white wine

250 ml cream

Few grates nutmeg

50 g Parmesan

Bunch parsley, finely chopped

This started off as a simple mushroom risotto, but it worked really well when made with the ancient, nutritious and super-tasty grain, quinoa, instead.

Serves 4

Rinse the quinoa well and the cook in plenty of boiling water for about 8 minutes and then drain, cool under running water and set aside. You could do this the day or night before which will make the serving of this dish very quick.

Heat up the olive oil and butter and sweat the onion until really soft and translucent. You could even put a lid on to stop it from colouring. Season well, add the mushrooms and garlic. Turn the heat up and then add the white wine. Let it cook off and evaporate so that the mixture becomes a little less wet. Then add the cream and again, keep the heat up and let it simmer and reduce a little. Add a few grates of nutmeg and then add the cooked quinoa. Mix well, and when good and hot, taste and season. Add the Parmesan and parsley; you can also sharpen it up with a little lemon juice. Serve in big bowls with extra Parmesan.

The quinoa really seems to keep absorbing all the liquid, so although it seems like quite a lot of liquid in this recipe, you'll be surprised how much it takes in. If you feel you want a 'looser' type of dish, simply let it down with another splash of cream or a little water.

96

tasty tostadas

400 g tinned black beans,
drained and rinsed

100 g crème fraîche

50 g grated cheddar

1 bunch spring onions, finely
sliced

Salt and pepper

Few splashes Tabasco

1 pinch ground cumin

4 corn tortillas

Olive oil

1 avocado

2 limes

4 eggs

Bunch coriander

These tostadas are immensely satisfying and reasonably healthy. They would be even better for you if you left out the crème fraîche, made a nice tomato salsa to garnish and poached the egg. They make a great brunch dish, but would happily do for dinner too.

Serves 4

Preheat the oven to 190°C. Mix the black beans in a food processor or mash them with a potato masher. You don't want to make them a purée, just crushed. Mix with the crème fraîche, cheddar and spring onions. Season with salt, pepper, some Tabasco and cumin. Set aside.

Cut the corn tortillas into smaller circles about the size of a fried egg. Take the trimmings and tear into large strips. Put the strips on a baking tray, drizzle with some olive oil, salt, pepper and a little ground cumin. (You can also add some cumin seeds or any other dried herbs and spices you like – even some smoked paprika would be good.) Bake them for about 10 minutes until golden brown and starting to crisp and dry out. Set aside to serve later as a garnish on top.

The rest is about assembly. When you are ready to serve, spoon equal quantities of the black bean mix onto the small tortilla rounds on a baking tray and bake for about 10–15 minutes until hot.

Meanwhile, peel and slice the avocado into nice half-moon slices and squirt with some lime juice. Fry your eggs in some olive oil and then plate up: top the beans with a fried egg and slices of avocado (or the other way around) and sprinkle with coriander, the baked tortilla crisps and a squeeze of lime juice. Some Tabasco also helps.

97

celeriac purée with black beans and rich onions

1 head celeriac, peeled and cut into chunks

2 knobs butter

1 tbsp Greek yoghurt

2 onions, peeled and sliced

1 tbsp olive oil

Tiny squeeze honey

400 g tinned black beans, drained and rinsed

2 cloves garlic, peeled and crushed

Pinch chilli flakes

Small bunch fresh coriander, chopped

This recipe features caramelised onions, the foundation for some classic dishes, the most well-known being French onion soup. This time they're partnered with black beans and set to rest on a soft, rich mash of creamy celeriac. Easy and quick to prepare, this is the perfect midweek vegetarian supper.

Serves 2 as a main course

Boil the chunks of celeriac till tender, then drain and blitz in a blender with one knob of butter and the yoghurt. In a pan, fry the onions with the olive oil and the second knob of butter until golden brown and sizzling; you don't want them to burn, just to brown, so this bit needs a little bit of care. Add a squeeze of honey to help this process along. Then add the black beans and garlic to the onions, cook for 5 minutes until heated through and season well.

Season the celeriac purée with the chilli flakes and chopped coriander and serve warm with a generous scoop of the bean and onion mix on top.

soba noodle salad

2 heads broccoli

Few glugs rapeseed or sunflower oil

Salt and pepper

Approx. 500 g tofu, diced

2 dessertspoons sesame oil

2 dessertspoons hoisin sauce

2 dessertspoons rice wine vinegar

3 preserved lemons, finely chopped

2 cloves garlic, peeled and crushed

3-inch piece ginger, peeled and grated

100 ml olive or sunflower oil

500 g soba noodles

4–6 sheets nori

2 tbsp sesame seeds, with extra to serve

2 bunches spring onions, sliced

To bulk this up and make it saltier and crunchier, you could add a handful of lightly chopped salted peanuts or black sesame seeds. In Asian markets, they also sell bags of crispy fried shallots, which would be perfect for something like this.

Serves 6

Preheat the oven to 190–200°C. Break the broccoli into small florets, toss with some oil and season with salt and pepper. Put in a roasting tray and cook for about 15–20 minutes until slightly charred and tender. Set aside. Dice the tofu and fry in oil in a non-stick frying pan until golden brown and season well. Set aside.

Make the dressing by mixing the sesame oil, hoisin, rice wine vinegar, preserved lemons, garlic and ginger. Whisk in the olive oil, though feel free to use sunflower oil instead. Season well or adjust the seasoning by adding in some soy sauce, chilli sauce or anything else you like.

Cook the soba noodles in boiling water for about 4 minutes, drain and rinse. They don't need to be completely cold. Hold the nori over a flame from a little height so that it toasts lightly. Then tear it up. Toss the well-drained noodles with the dressing first. Then add the sesame seeds, spring onions, broccoli and nori. Mix well, season and serve with extra sesame seeds on top.

courgette, pine nut and ricotta tart

2 tbsp olive oil

3–4 courgettes (approx. 1 kg in total)

Salt and pepper

500 g ricotta

4 eggs, beaten

Large handful basil, roughly torn

Grate nutmeg

150 g Parmesan

1–2 cloves garlic, peeled and crushed

500 g puff pastry

Flour for dusting

Large handful pine nuts

This tart will stay tasty even after a day or two in the fridge. It shouldn't go soggy, though it won't be quite as crisp and delicious as if consumed on the day it's made.

Makes 12 generous slices

Preheat the oven to 200°C. Heat up the olive oil in a decent-sized frying pan and slice the courgettes thinly. Sweat them in the oil on a medium to low heat and season well. When they are soft, set aside to cool. Mix the ricotta, eggs, basil, nutmeg and 50 g Parmesan, along with the garlic. You can do this with a whisk, spoon or electric beater. Season this mixture also.

On a lightly floured surface, roll out the puff pastry so that it is slightly larger than a standard baking tray. Then fold over the edges to form a little rim and slightly crimp the pastry. Slide the baking tray (the kind with no edges) under the pastry and put back in the fridge.

When the courgettes have cooled down, spread the ricotta mixture on top of the pastry and smooth with a spatula. Layer the courgettes on top and then sprinkle the pine nuts and remaining 100 g grated Parmesan on top of that. Bake for about 35–40 minutes until slightly puffed up and a lovely golden brown. Allow it to cool down, slice and serve. Otherwise, cool down fully, refrigerate and serve cold the next day. It's also fine to reheat at about 180°C for 15 minutes or so.

caramelised garlic tart

500 g puff pastry, defrosted

3 heads garlic, peeled

2 tbsp olive oil

2 tbsp balsamic vinegar

220 ml water

1 tbsp caster sugar

1 tbsp rosemary and thyme, chopped

Salt and pepper

120 g soft goat's cheese, crumbled

120 g hard goat's cheese, roughly chopped

3 eggs

200 g crème fraîche

This tart is a variation on a lovely Yotam Ottolenghi recipe. It's a must for when you want to eat something vegetarian and delicious and have an hour or two to enjoy making and cooking it. You can use any type of goat's cheese, but if you use some hard and some soft, you get a great balance of textures.

Serves 4

Preheat the oven to 180°C. Roll out the puff pastry so that it lines the base and sides of a 28 cm tart tin. If you have the time, stick it in the fridge for 20 minutes or so to rest. Then prick the base with a fork and line the pastry with greaseproof paper and dried beans or rice.

'Blind bake' the pastry like this for 25 minutes, then carefully remove the paper and beans and put back in the oven for another 5 minutes so that the base dries out. Set aside to cool. Turn the oven down to 160°C.

Sweat the whole garlic cloves in the olive oil over a very gentle heat for 10 minutes, but don't allow them to colour. Then turn up the heat and add the balsamic vinegar, water and sugar. Simmer gently for 10 minutes, then add the herbs and season with salt and pepper. Most of the liquid needs to evaporate so the cloves become well coated in a dark, caramelly, thick glaze. Set aside.

Scatter the cheeses onto the base of the pastry. Then scatter the garlic cloves and any of the balsamic juices on top, arranging the cloves so that they are evenly distributed. Whisk the eggs and crème fraîche and pour on top.

Bake the tart on a baking tray (so it's easier to transport) at 160°C for about 35 minutes or so until the mixture looks as though it has just set – there's not that much liquid in this recipe, so it does cook quickly. Allow to cool slightly before slicing and serving with a big salad.

feta, date and sweet corn fritters

2 tbsp olive oil

2 tsp fennel seeds

2 tsp cumin seeds

1 tsp turmeric

Pinch chilli flakes

2 red onions, peeled and very finely diced

2 cloves garlic, peeled and crushed

Salt and pepper

1 good tsp sugar

170–200 g feta, finely diced

200 g stoned dates, finely chopped

2 bunches spring onions, very finely sliced

Approx. 300 g tinned sweetcorn, drained, or kernels from 2 corn on the cob

170 g flour

75 g polenta

¹/₂ tsp bicarbonate of soda

³/₄ tsp baking powder

100 ml yoghurt and 50 ml milk or 150 ml buttermilk

2 eggs

Sunflower or rapeseed oil for frying

This fritter recipe seemed a bit daunting at first and full of ingredients you would rarely keep stocked, such as buttermilk and chickpea flour. So after some dabbling and simplifying, you can get a great result with a little more ease. These are a big hit with everyone and taste great as a nibble for a large gathering of friends. Kids should even go for them. They can also be reheated the next day.

Serves 8 – makes about 28–30 fritters

Heat the olive oil in a frying pan and fry the fennel and cumin seeds, turmeric and chilli flakes until starting to smell good and strong. Add the red onions and garlic and cook until starting to caramelize. Then season and add the sugar. Caramelise a bit more and then put in a bowl and let it cool down.

Meanwhile, dice the feta, dates and spring onions. Add these to the red onion mix along with the corn kernels. Set aside to cool.

Put the flour, polenta, soda and baking powder in a bowl. Mix the milk and yoghurt or buttermilk with the eggs. Make a well in the dry ingredients and pour in the egg and milk mixture. Mix with a wooden spoon until it becomes a thick batter and then add in the spiced vegetables and cheese. The batter will be like thick porridge. Put a plate covered in paper towels nearby to drain the fritters. Heat up 1 cm of oil in a large, non-stick frying pan and fry dessert-spoonfuls of the batter. They cook quite quickly, so turn them over so they fry on both sides, and drain on the paper towels. Do them in batches and either serve while still warm or let them cool down and reheat the next day.

sweet potato, spinach and feta frittata

300 g sweet potato (1–2, depending on size)

80 ml olive oil

Salt and black pepper

1 red onion, peeled and sliced

Little squeeze honey or pinch sugar

Approx. 120 g baby spinach

Approx. 200 g feta, diced

12 eggs, beaten

2–3 tbsp Greek yoghurt

1 clove garlic, peeled and crushed

Few pinches sumac/smoked sweet paprika

The clever thing about this very tasty frittata, adapted from a Peter Gordon recipe, is putting a little blob of Greek yoghurt with a sprinkle of sumac on top. It gives a delicious richness to a dish that can be quite dry if overcooked. If you don't have sumac, a little smoked sweet paprika or some black pepper would also work. The sweet potatoes also give it bulk and a certain wetness, ensuring a soft and tasty frittata.

Serves 4–6 (or 20 tapas-style treats)

Preheat the oven to 180°C. Chop up the sweet potato into small, dice-sized pieces, skin and all, and put onto parchment paper on a roasting tray. Pour over about ¼ of the olive oil, season well and roast for about 20 minutes until they are just starting to brown and are tender.

In a large ovenproof frying pan, sweat the red onion with the remaining olive oil and season well. Do this very slowly and add a little honey to accentuate the sweetness. Add the spinach, let it wilt slightly and then take off the heat.

Scatter the cooked sweet potatoes on top of the spinach along with the feta. Give the frying pan a cursory stir and then add the beaten eggs. You need to poke the mixture to make sure all the goodies are evenly distributed and that the egg can permeate all the nooks and crannies. Then bake in the oven until firm. This can take about 25–30 minutes, but remember that the egg will keep on cooking as it cools down.

This tastes great at room temperature with some of the flavoured Greek yoghurt. Make by simply mixing the garlic and Greek yoghurt with some salt and pepper and then sprinkling with sumac or smoked sweet paprika.

103

thyme, onion and Gruyère tart

For the pastry:
130 g butter
200 g flour
1–2 tbsp iced water

For the filling:
100 g butter
1.3 kg Spanish onions
(approx. 6) peeled and sliced
Salt and pepper
250 ml double cream
1 heaped tbsp Dijon mustard
Few sprigs thyme
2 eggs, beaten
4 egg yolks, beaten
200 g Gruyère, grated

Not all cheeses can stand up to heat like Gruyère, but it really comes into its own when added to hot dishes, especially when eggs, thyme and sweated onions are concerned. Rich and delicious, this is everything you want from a savoury tart. It's vegetarian, full of tasty fats and really does only need a crisp salad and a glass of something cool and crisp to go along side. You will need a 27-cm tart tin with a removable base. I adore this tart.

Serves 8–10

In a food processor, mix the butter and flour. When it's formed fine crumbs, add in enough water for it to form a ball, then wrap the pastry in cling film and chill down for an hour in the fridge while you get started on the filling. Preheat the oven to 180°C.

Melt the butter in heavy-based saucepan with a snug lid and sweat the onions slowly for at least 25 minutes. They'll need to the odd stir and should shrink down by at least half. Try not to colour them. The steam that gets trapped in the saucepan and the low heat should help keep them sweating rather than sautéing. Season really well, then remove from the heat and allow to cool down.

Roll out your pastry between two sheets of parchment paper. You won't have a lot of excess pastry. Line the tart case with the pastry, and then cover with scrunched up parchment paper – scrunching it up just makes it more pliable – and fill with dried beans and bake for about 25 minutes. Carefully remove the paper and beans and then cook for another few minutes to dry out the tart shell.

By this stage, the onions should be cool enough. Add the cream, Dijon mustard and thyme and stir well. Then add in the eggs and egg yolks. Season lightly and then mix in about a third of the Gruyère. Put the tart case on a baking tray to make it easier to transport. Fill the tart case with the onions first so that you can distribute them evenly, and then ladle or spoon in the liquid.

Don't overfill it, as it will leak all over the oven. Sprinkle the Gruyère on top and bake for 20 minutes by which stage you may be able to top up with a little more filling. Bake until just set which takes about 35–40 minutes in total. Let it cool down and rest. It will keep on cooking. This is best served whilst still warm or room temp.

butternut squash 'steaks' with labneh and beetroot salsa

500 g natural yoghurt
Salt and pepper
Lemon juice
1 butternut squash
Olive oil
Few sprigs fresh thyme, chopped

For the beetroot salsa:
4 small to medium fresh beetroots (not pickled), peeled and grated (you can grate them in a food processor)

1 red chilli, deseeded and finely chopped

Big bunch parsley, finely chopped

For the dressing:
120 ml olive oil
60 ml balsamic

These 'steaks' are quite fancy and would be perfect as a vegetarian main course for a dinner party or just for a midweek treat. Removing and toasting the seeds is not compulsory, but will make you feel that bit more accomplished.

Labneh is simply Greek yoghurt that has been left to strain through muslin overnight, which gives the yoghurt a thicker, more cheese-like consistency. It's delicious with some lemon juice, light seasoning and chopped fresh herbs. Note that you have to start the labneh the day before.

Serves 4

Strain the yoghurt through muslin overnight, discard the liquid and season the solids (the labneh) with salt, pepper, lemon juice and whatever chopped fresh herbs you fancy.

Preheat the oven to 200°C. Wash and dry the squash, lay it on its side, cut off the ends and slice into 4 to 6 1-inch-thick rounds, or 'steaks', leaving the skin on and removing the seeds. This next bit is optional: toast the seeds in the oven on a tray for about 15 minutes or until lightly browned. Alternatively, you can toast a mix of seeds – sunflower and pumpkin is a great combination – for the same use. Set aside for later.

Place the squash steaks on a baking tray lined with parchment, drizzle with olive oil, season lightly and sprinkle the chopped thyme over the top. Bake in the oven for about 40–45 minutes.

To make the salsa, mix together the grated beetroot, chilli and parsley in a bowl and dress with the olive oil and balsamic vinegar.

To serve, sprinkle the toasted seeds over the steaks and serve with a large spoonful of the salsa and a dollop of soothing labneh.

nut loaf

150 g almonds, with the skin on

100 g hazelnuts (preferably with no skin, but fine if with skins)

50 g shelled pistachios

4 medium carrots, peeled and grated

3 medium leeks, washed and very finely chopped

1 large onion, peeled and finely chopped

1 tbsp fresh thyme leaves

2 cloves garlic, peeled and finely chopped

2–3 tbsp olive oil

Very large bunch parsley

2 eggs

100 g strong, hard cheese, such as goat's

Some people will associate nut loaf with Christmas – the option usually adopted for visiting vegetarians – but this dish is so good you'll want to enjoy it throughout the year. The recipe, which is the result of much experimenting, is full of flavour, gluten-free and so moist it doesn't even need gravy. You'll need a 30 cm x 10 cm loaf tin for this.

Serves 6–8

Preheat the oven to 150°C. Toast the nuts in the oven on a tray for ten minutes at about 150°C, taking care not to burn them. Take them out and turn the oven up to 170°C.

Heat the olive oil in a large, heavy pan and sweat the carrots, leeks, onion, thyme and garlic together until soft but not coloured, which should take about 15 minutes.

Next, blitz the nuts and parsley in a food processor. When they have formed a sandy 'crumb', add the eggs and cheese. Mix this with the sweated vegetables and pour into a lined loaf tin. Bake at 170°C for 30–40 minutes until firm. Serve thick slices warm, or let it cool down fully and serve cold.

stuffed peppers with sweet potato and chestnuts

1 large sweet potato, diced

2 tbsp olive or coconut oil

1 red onion, peeled and finely sliced

1 clove garlic, peeled and crushed

200 g cooked, peeled chestnuts, chopped

12 cherry tomatoes, halved

1 tsp thyme leaves

Pinch chilli flakes

1 egg, beaten

4 red peppers, cut in half, pith and seeds removed but stems intact (this stops the peppers from collapsing in the oven)

Few chunks of goat's cheese

Chopped parsley

These stuffed peppers are a substantial vegetarian main course. Sometimes, the key to good vegetarian cooking is getting the texture as well as the flavour just right, and this dish has got both thanks to the chestnuts. You can also make it vegan if you omit the egg and cheese; it will still be super tasty.

Serves 4

Preheat the oven to 180°C. Cook the diced sweet potato in half the oil on a parchment-lined baking tray for 15 minutes or until tender.

Meanwhile, sweat the onion and garlic in the rest of the oil until soft but not coloured, which should take about 10 minutes.

In a bowl, mix the onion and sweet potato with the chestnuts, tomatoes, thyme, garlic and chilli flakes. Add in the beaten egg to bind it.

Stuff the peppers with the mixture and top with a generous sprinkling of goat's cheese. Bake for 30 minutes. Serve with a green salad.

roasted aubergine with hummus and aubergine 'smash'

1 aubergine, sliced into 1-cm-thick rounds (about 6–8 slices)

3–4 tbsp olive oil

1 tsp dried rosemary

2 cloves garlic, peeled and chopped

400 g tinned chickpeas, drained and rinsed

Juice of half a lemon

Salt and pepper

1 tsp cumin seeds

¹/₂ tsp dried thyme

This dish is easy to make and is one of those vegetarian dishes that is made more robust and 'meaty' thanks to aubergine, a vegetable that is transformed by heat and time from something very bland into rich flesh bursting with a complex, almost smoky flavour. That flavour really comes through in the 'smash' which is made by mixing whole and smashed chickpeas with aubergines that have been roasted with oil, herbs, spices and garlic and then whizzed in a blender with the chickpeas.

Very Middle Eastern, very simple and very tasty.

Serves 2

Preheat the oven to 180°C. Brush the aubergine well with olive oil, season and sprinkle with half the rosemary and the garlic. Bake for 15–20 minutes until golden brown and just tender, making sure to turn them over halfway through.

When cooked, keep about half the slices of aubergine and set aside. Blitz the other half of the cooked aubergines together with half the chickpeas in a blender with olive oil, the lemon juice and salt and pepper. Add more lemon juice if it's not tangy enough.

Meanwhile, roast the remainder of the chickpeas in the oven with the rest of the rosemary the cumin, thyme and salt and pepper, for about 10–15 minutes. You can put the aubergine slices back in for a few minutes to heat up. To serve, place a blob of the 'smash' on top of the sliced cooked aubergine and sprinkle with the oven-roasted chickpeas.

aubergine, courgette and basil gratin

2–3 aubergines

Olive oil

Salt and pepper

4 courgettes

2 red onions, peeled and sliced

Few sprigs thyme

4 cloves garlic, peeled and crushed

4 large tomatoes, roughly chopped or 1–2 tins tomatoes

3 tbsp red wine vinegar

Fresh basil leaves

100 g Parmesan, grated

Few dots crème fraîche (optional)

This aubergine and courgette gratin is one I love because simply because it's vegetarian, quick, cheap, easy and everyone in the family happily eats it.

Serves 4–6

Preheat the oven to 180°C. Cut the aubergine into small cubes and sauté in a large saucepan with the olive oil and plenty of salt and pepper. You'll probably have to add more olive oil than you like, but if you're trying to stay slim, add a splash of water instead to help keep it cooking.

Meanwhile, slice the courgette with a potato peeler (or as thin as you can) and then toss with olive oil, salt and pepper. Set aside.

Add the onion and thyme to the aubergine. Keep cooking out and then add the garlic. Try to get some colour on the aubergines before adding in the tomatoes and vinegar. Keep the heat up, cook out and reduce slightly. Taste and adjust the seasoning. Add in half the grated Parmesan and pour into a gratin dish.

Top with the thin slices of courgette and sprinkle the remaining Parmesan on top and then bake for about 45 minutes. If you want to make it a bit more lavish, you can dot some crème fraîche on top along with the cheese, but it's not necessary. Let it settle for a few minutes before eating.

black bean chilli

Olive oil

4 cloves garlic, peeled and crushed

2 red onions, peeled and finely sliced

1 tsp chilli powder

2 tsp ground cumin

1 tbsp dried oregano

2 tsp instant coffee

Pinch sugar or squeeze honey

800 g tinned chopped tomatoes

1 cinnamon stick

400 g tinned black beans, drained

To serve:

4 corn tortilla wraps, ripped into triangles

Olive oil

Herbs and spices

Bunch spring onions, finely sliced

Bunch coriander, chopped

Few spoons of crème fraîche

Good Mexican and Tex-Mex dishes are always crowd-pleasers. Whether it's for a midweek supper or a weekend brunch, this black bean chilli is versatile, quick to prepare and very, very tasty, especially if you go the whole hog and lay on the accompanying bits and bobs.

Serves 4

Preheat the oven to 160°C. Sauté the garlic and onions in olive oil until very soft and starting to colour, which should only take about 10 minutes. Add the chilli, cumin, oregano, coffee and sugar and stir. Then add the tomatoes and cinnamon and simmer for 20 minutes. Finally, add the black beans, let them heat through, adjust the seasoning and you're ready to go.

Drizzle tortillas with olive oil and season with herbs and spices. Bake in the oven until crisp.

Serve with the tortilla crisps and condiments above, and feel free to make some guacamole to add to the proceedings.

110

Catriona and Lina's torta verde

100 g Arborio rice

1 packet filo pastry, defrosted

2 onions, peeled and finely chopped

Olive oil

500 g frozen spinach, thawed and drained

150 g Parmesan, grated

Few grates nutmeg

Salt and pepper

100 g melted butter

Italians are famously secretive when it comes to sharing recipes, but my sister-in-law secretly shared her Italian mother-in-law's recipe for this Ligurian classic. Torta verde (literally 'green tart') is a pie of spinach, Arborio rice and Parmesan cocooned in buttered sheets of pastry and baked till crisp and golden.

I swap the shortcrust for some filo and use frozen spinach instead of the Swiss chard and fresh spinach, which can be a bit bulky. Often, spinach can rob pastry of its crispness, but here the rice cleverly absorbs any juices, so what you get is a lovely dry, flavoursome pie.

Lovely for lunch or supper and just as nice the next day.

Serves 8–10

Preheat the oven to 200°C. Cook the rice in boiling water until al dente. Drain and set aside.

Next, sweat the onions in 2 good glugs of olive oil in a large frying pan until soft. Add the drained spinach and the rice and cook out until nice and dry. Take off the heat, add the Parmesan and a few grates of nutmeg and season well.

Take a loose-bottomed tart tin, about 28 cm across, and line it with the filo, taking care to leave a generous overhang of about 15 cm all around. Generously butter each sheet one at a time as it goes in. Add the spinach filling and then fold the overhanging sheets over the pie, as if wrapping a present (badly).

To finish, crumple another 1 to 2 sheets of filo and place over the top, generously painting with more melted butter and bake in the oven for 20–30 minutes until golden brown. Eat warm or cold.

quinoa, cauliflower, raisin and feta cakes

200 g quinoa
$^1/_2$ head cauliflower
1 bunch spring onions, finely sliced
2 cloves garlic, peeled and crushed
4 eggs, beaten
200 g feta cheese, crumbled
50 g raisins, chopped
1 large bunch coriander or flat-leaf parsley, chopped
80 g rolled oats
Salt and pepper
Olive oil

These quinoa cakes are really nice and the perfect way to use up quinoa if you've prepared too much for a salad. They are also a great snack, even cold and straight from the fridge. You can also throw most bits of leftover veg in here, especially sweet potato and even broccoli. The olive salsa is not obligatory, but good if you're looking to beef things up a bit.

Serves 12 (12 cakes)

Cook the quinoa by simmering gently in boiling water for 15 minutes. Drain and let it cool down and continue draining. You could also do this the day before.

Put the cauliflower in a food processor and mix on pulse until it resembles fine breadcrumbs. Add it to the quinoa and add the rest of the other ingredients (except the olive oil) and mix really well. Then shape into 12 patties and put on a baking tray or similar and chill in the fridge for at least 30 minutes. Again, you could leave them overnight.

To cook, preheat your oven to 180°C. Fry them in batches in the olive oil until golden brown on both sides and then transfer to a baking tray and cook for another 10 minutes in the oven. Eat warm or cold.

quick olive salsa

4 tbsp tapenade
1 clove garlic, peeled and crushed
2 tbsp raisins, chopped
Small bunch chopped flat-leaf parsley
Squeeze honey or agave syrup
1–2 tsp sherry or balsamic vinegar

Mix all the ingredients together and chill until ready to serve. Give it a good mix and spoon onto each plate.

112

beetroot carpaccio with honeyed walnuts and Roquefort cheese

4 raw beetroots, peeled and sliced on a mandolin (or just thinly sliced)

Few splashes red wine vinegar

Scant tbsp olive oil

100 g walnuts

Splash walnut oil or olive oil

Few rosemary sprigs, stripped and roughly chopped

Few thyme sprigs, stripped and roughly chopped

2–3 tbsp honey

100 g Roquefort, loosely crumbled

Watercress to garnish

This beetroot salad is full of texture and winning flavours that combine beautifully. With the rich brilliance of the beetroot, it also looks stunning. The wafer-thin disks are the result of an encounter with a mandolin, a steel slicing tool not unlike a grater.

Serves 5

Marinate the sliced raw beetroot in the vinegar and oil and season with a little salt. This will 'cook' it. Leave aside until you're ready to plate up.

Next, toast the walnuts for 5 to 10 minutes on a roasting tray in the oven at about 150°C, then set them aside to cool. Season the nuts with the oil, rosemary, thyme, salt and pepper and honey.

To assemble the salad, arrange the beetroot slices on the plate – a bit haphazard looks best – and scatter the cheese and walnuts over the top. Garnish with some watercress and drizzles of olive oil.

113

cauliflower, courgette and goat's cheese pizza

For the base:

1 head cauliflower

Approx. 200 g soft goat's cheese

1 egg

1 tsp dried thyme

For the sauce:

Good glug olive oil

4 cloves garlic, peeled and crushed

1 onion, peeled and diced

1 red pepper, cored and roughly chopped

Pinch chilli flakes

400 g tinned chopped tomatoes

1–2 tsp dried oregano

2 bay leaves

Pinch smoked sweet paprika or cayenne pepper

Salt and pepper

For the topping:

1 courgette

Olive oil

Salt and pepper

Approx. 100 g of your favourite goat's cheese

This is another recipe from Doris Choi, the New-York-based raw food chef (and my sister-in-law!), who teamed up with raw food guru Natalia Rose to produce the Fresh Energy Cookbook. It might sound a bit unappetising but this cauliflower pizza really is superb. It is very moreish and surprisingly filling and it tastes even better when it cools down to room temperature.

Serves 4–6

To make the base, remove the green stalks from the cauliflower (these are good when you're roasting cauliflower, but don't work here!) and cut or break the florets into small pieces. Blend in a food processor on pulse mode until you make white 'breadcrumbs' that look a little damp. Don't over-process to a pulp, but do make sure it's fully ground up.

Then in a large bowl, mix the crumbs with the goat's cheese, thyme and egg. It's almost like beating sugar and butter together with no electric beater. You can do it just with a spatula and it's easier if the cheese is soft and at room temperature. Eventually you will feel that everything is reasonably well distributed.

Get a baking tray or brownie tin and generously line with parchment paper. Then spread the 'dough' onto the paper and pat down with the spatula. Put another sheet of parchment over it and smooth out the cauliflower with the palms of your hands so that it spreads out to about ½-inch thick. It's almost like Play-Doh, and you can push it into the corners. You can chill and set aside or even overnight while the sauce is cooking away.

When you are ready, cook the pizza base on its own for about 20 minutes at 200°C. It will start out looking a little pale but will go golden on top. Lift up the paper to check the underneath is OK. The edges may char a bit, but this is fine. Set aside to cool down.

To make the sauce, heat up the olive oil and sweat the garlic, onion and red pepper. Do this for a few minutes. Add the rest of the ingredients and simmer over gentle heat for about 20 minutes. Then remove the bay leaf. When it has cooled down, blitz until smooth in a blender. This will make too much sauce, but it can be frozen in batches so you have some ready to go next time you want a home-made pizza sauce that's a bit fruitier than normal.

For the topping, cut the courgette on a mandolin, with a potato peeler or very finely with a knife. Toss with a little olive oil and salt and pepper. When you are ready to do the final 10 minutes of cooking, spread a few tablespoons of sauce onto the pizza base, then top with slivers of courgette and scatter some goat's cheese on top. Bake for another 10 minutes until the cheese is just starting to melt. Allow to cool and settle and serve. Just as good cold, if not better!

PASTA AND PIZZA

114

orzo with prawns, leeks and lemon

100 ml olive oil

2 leeks, sliced using as much of the green parts as possible

5 cloves garlic, peeled and chopped

2 tsp fennel seeds

100 g butter

Salt and pepper

400 g frozen prawns

Juice of 1 lemon

1 glass white wine

Pinch chilli flakes

Pinch sugar

500 g orzo

This is a great example of an easy-to-prepare dish that uses jarred or frozen staples you should have around the kitchen, so you can whip up a casual fork supper at a moment's notice. Orzo, that small, silky and slippery little pasta, which is more like rice than your ordinary pasta, is really luscious to eat. The prawn, leek and lemon sauce is light and zingy enough not to overload the pasta and can be made in a jiffy. Orzo pasta is always nicer with a light, blonde sauce, as it tends to disappear when you serve it with something tomato-based or too heavy. If you don't have orzo, use whatever small pasta you can find. You can use raw or cooked prawns, but just adjust the cooking time as appropriate. It's super tasty, quick and very satisfying.

Serves 6

Put a big pot of water on to boil for the pasta, and get on with making the sauce.

Heat the olive oil in a large, heavy-based saucepan, and sweat the leeks and garlic, but don't colour them. Add the fennel seeds and butter, and then season well. Add the prawns in frozen. Put the lid on and let the steam and heat from the leeks cook them until they are a cute shade of pink and piping hot. They are a bit rubbery, but this is all about flavour, so don't get heartbroken, as they certainly won't be golden brown and sizzling. Throw in the lemon juice and glass of wine and season with chilli flakes and sugar. Check the seasoning.

Meanwhile, your big pot of water will be boiling. Cook the orzo (according to the packet, but it's pretty quick), then drain, add a splash of olive oil and add to the leek sauce. Mix well and serve.

115

spaghetti with no-cook tomato sauce

400 g cherry tomatoes

Good pinch sea salt

1 tsp caster sugar

Lots of black pepper

50 ml olive oil

2 cloves garlic, peeled and crushed

1 tsp rosemary leaves, finely chopped

1 tbsp red wine vinegar

50 g pitted black olives, roughly chopped

Small bunch basil, roughly chopped

200 g spaghetti

This tomato sauce makes for a fantastic, quick, vegetarian supper either as a no-cook pasta sauce or simply as a tomato salad.

Serves 2

Cut the tomatoes in half and put them in a good-sized bowl with the salt, sugar, pepper, olive oil, garlic, rosemary and red wine vinegar. Leave it to sit and macerate for anything up to an hour at room temperature. Taste it and adjust the seasoning. When ready to serve, cook the pasta in plenty of boiling water, drain and toss with a little extra olive oil and season lightly. Mix the sauce with the pasta in the same saucepan and the residual heat will warm the sauce through. Serve immediately.

116

wholewheat spaghetti with olives, capers and herbs

Approx. 250 g pitted kalamata olives

Large bunch parsley

Large bunch mint

2 tbsp capers

2 cloves garlic, peeled and crushed

200 ml olive oil

Salt and pepper

500 g wholewheat spaghetti

This comes from an American book called Ancient Grains and is made with wholewheat spaghetti, which is healthier to eat than regular pasta. If there's a good enough sauce on it, you can usually pretend it's plain pasta. This sauce is very much a 'store cupboard' one and is really delicious. The spaghetti also made a nice supper on day two.

Serves 4

Roughly chop the olives and herbs and mix together in a decent-sized bowl, crush the capers with the back of a knife and add in along with the garlic. Whisk or stir in the olive oil and season really well. You could also add some lemon zest to this. Leave it at room temperature so the flavours develop.

Boil up the pasta, drain well and then toss with the sauce. Serve warm rather than piping hot.

117

spaghetti with crab and mint

125 ml olive oil

50 g breadcrumbs

2 cloves garlic, peeled and crushed

2 pinches chilli flakes

Zest and juice of 2 lemons

Salt and pepper

350 g spaghetti

350 g cooked crab meat

Bunch mint, roughly chopped

Handful of watercress or rocket

This is based on a recipe by Lucas Hollweg. You could try it with coriander or just parsley, but his idea for using mint really appeals, particularly if the weather is getting warmer. There's something quite fragrant, light and summery about it.

Serves 4

This is a very quick dinner to make: in a frying pan, fry the breadcrumbs with about $1/3$ of the olive oil, the garlic and chilli, as well as the lemon zest. Season well. Shake the breadcrumbs about in the pan and let them brown slightly. Cook the pasta in plenty of boiling water, drain and stir in the last $2/3$ of the olive oil. Add the crab meat, mint and lemon juice, and toss. Season and pile into bowls. Top with the breadcrumbs and watercress or rocket.

pasta with chicken, peas and rosemary cream

100 ml cream

150 ml chicken stock

Zest and juice of 1 lemon

4 cloves garlic, peeled and chopped

4 sprigs rosemary and thyme

Big knob butter

Good glug or two of olive oil

4 chicken breasts, cut into strips

Salt and pepper

1 glass white wine

300 g frozen peas

Approx. 100 g Parmesan, grated

400 g macaroni

This dish is perfect for an evening when you want to invite a few friends around to dinner or need to feed a bunch of people with some very basic ingredients and not too much faffing around.

This is also the sort of thing you could prepare the night before and leave to cool before leaving overnight in the fridge. The chicken pieces can be sautéed in advance, then cooled right down and set aside in the fridge until you're ready to add them to the sauce and heat through till piping hot. This means it could be assembled in less than 10 minutes once you have your prep done.

Serves 4

Heat together the cream, chicken stock, lemon juice and zest, garlic, rosemary and thyme in a saucepan until simmering and let it bubble away gently until reduced by about half. Set aside. Heat up the butter and olive oil in a heavy-based frying pan and fry the chicken, possibly in two batches, until golden brown and cooked through. Season really well.

When you're finished cooking the chicken, add in the glass of wine to deglaze the pan and let it simmer and bubble away until it pretty much evaporates. Add the chicken to the cream sauce and keep warm. Cook the macaroni in boiling water, then drain and season. Put the pasta back in a large saucepan, mix with a small glug of olive oil and add the peas. Heat gently, adding the cream sauce and chicken. Mix everything together and season well. Spoon into bowl and top with a good sprinkling of Parmesan.

pasta pesto salad with spinach and peas

Approx. 450 g frozen spinach

4 tbsp pesto sauce

Juice of 1 lemon

2 tbsp mayonnaise

Approx. 50 ml olive oil

Salt and pepper

500 g pasta

200 g frozen peas

Handful pine nuts

Pasta pesto seems to be the one dish that kids would quite happily have for every single meal. There are worse things, of course, but it is sometimes handy to use it to get them to eat healthier food. Wholewheat pasta can sometimes be disguised by a really big dollop of pesto, a good knob of butter and a little Parmesan. This dish uses a full pack of spinach and could be a bit hard going, so maybe start with less and build up from there.

Serves 6 (and can be used for packed lunches)

Let the spinach thaw out and drain in a colander. When it's thawed, squeeze out excess moisture, or even better, squeeze dry in a tea towel. Then mix in a food processor along with the pesto, lemon juice, mayonnaise and a splash of olive oil. If you want to be mean (but nice), chuck in some raw garlic. Set aside till the pasta is ready.

Cook the pasta in plenty of boiling water until cooked and then drain. Give it a very brief rinse with some cold water, but don't let it get too chilly. Chuck it back in the hot saucepan, add the olive oil and frozen peas – the residual heat will cook them sufficiently. Season well. Mix with the pesto sauce and adjust the seasoning. It should also be fine for a couple of days in the fridge.

Lightly toast the pine nuts in the oven at about 160°C until they are a rich golden colour and sprinkle on top of the salad for extra crunch.

120

spaghetti with meatballs

400–600 g spaghetti

For the meatballs:
Olive oil
2 onions, peeled and finely diced
6 cloves garlic, peeled and chopped
1 tsp dried oregano
Salt and pepper
250 g sausage meat
200 g minced beef
100 g Parmesan, grated
1 egg, beaten
50 g breadcrumbs
Pinch nutmeg

For the tomato sauce:
50 ml olive oil
6 cloves garlic, peeled and sliced
1 bay leaf
1 tsp dried oregano
800 g tinned chopped tomatoes
Parmesan rind, optional
1 tbsp caster sugar
Splash of red wine

This recipe for meatballs is tasty because of the sausage meat, Parmesan, dried oregano and a simple but well-seasoned tomato sauce. Another advantage is that the meatballs and the sauce can be prepared the day before and then tossed with the cooked spaghetti at the last minute.

Serves 4

Heat up a few glugs of the olive oil in a large frying pan and sweat the onions and garlic slowly and gently until very soft. Then transfer them to a bowl and let them cool fully before mixing in a food processor (or by hand using lots of elbow grease) with the rest of the ingredients.

Shape into small golf balls and chill for 10 minutes or overnight. Heat up another few glugs of olive, preferably in a non-stick frying pan oil and fry the meatballs until dark brown all over (about 10 minutes). Keep warm while you cook the tomato sauce.

Heat up the olive oil and sweat the garlic along with the bay leaf, oregano and then add the tinned tomatoes. Season with the sugar, salt and pepper and add a Parmesan rind for extra flavour if you have one.

Add the red wine and simmer gently for 20 minutes, occasionally stirring making sure it's not burning because of the sugar. The Parmesan rind can be rinsed off and used again or else chucked away.

To assemble, add the meatballs to the hot tomato sauce and heat thoroughly while you cook the spaghetti in big saucepan of boiling salted water, to which you've added a splash of olive oil. Cook until al dente, drain and toss with another couple of tablespoons of olive oil. Season the spaghetti and then dish out and spoon over the tomato sauce and meatballs.

summer comfort fettuccine

4 tbsp olive oil, plus an extra glug

2 red onions, peeled and very finely chopped

3 cloves garlic, peeled and crushed

100 g sundried tomatoes, drained and finely chopped

250 ml vegetable stock or water

1 large glass white wine

Good pinch chilli flakes

350 g fettuccine

250 ml cream

Approx. 750 g frozen raw prawns

Salt and pepper

100 g Parmesan, finely grated

Approx. 100 g baby spinach

Big knob butter

Big bunch basil, chopped

This pasta dish is pretty rich and creamy and therefore falls into the summer comfort category and is always very popular. It contains some chopped up sundried tomatoes, which always add a little sparkle to dishes. You can use raw, frozen prawns, but they could just as easily be left out for vegetarians – just add a few more sundried tomatoes, or sauté some courgettes separately and add them in instead of the frozen prawns.

Serves 4

Sweat the olive oil and red onions along with the garlic until soft but not coloured. Add the chopped sundried tomatoes, the vegetable stock or water along with the wine and chilli flakes. Simmer for 5 minutes until bubbling and reduced slightly. At this stage, you can boil the pasta. While the pasta is cooking, add the cream to the sauce and then add in the frozen prawns. Keep the heat up high and cook until the prawns turn pink and are cooked through. Season well. Add the Parmesan, spinach and mix until wilted. Feel free to add a squeeze of lemon juice if it needs to be sharpened up.

Drain the pasta, toss with the butter, basil and a splash of olive oil, season lightly and then mix with the sauce and serve.

122

pasta with salami, tomato cream and rocket

200 g orecchiette (or penne) pasta

4 tbsp olive oil

2 red onions, peeled and sliced

Approx. 100 g spicy salami

Pinch chilli flakes

Approx. 150 g cherry tomatoes, cut into quarters

Salt and black pepper

2 cloves garlic, peeled and minced

1 glass white wine

100 ml cream

2 good handfuls rocket

Grated Parmesan to serve

This recipe involves a little sautéing (gentle frying) and then a little reduction (simmering with intent) and is extremely easy to execute, even for reluctant chefs. The recipe has a little cream and white wine, which is the basis of many a good dish: cream and wine reductions that lead to a tasty sauce that is always a little more complex in taste than you'd expect. It's that wonderful alchemy that happens when you intensify flavours and add a splash of alcohol. Food just livens up.

Serves 4 as starter, 2 as a main course

Start the sauce before cooking the pasta, but do get the water on to boil for it first. Heat up half the olive oil in a decent-sized frying pan and cook the onions over a high enough heat so that they start to get a little colour on them. Chop up the salami into small chunks and add in. The fat will start to render down and the salami should start to crisp up. Add the chilli flakes.

To calm down the browning action, slop all of the chopped cherry tomatoes into the pan and season really well. Add the garlic, turn up the heat and then add the wine and cook off so that a good bit of liquid starts to evaporate. Then add the cream and simmer for a couple more minutes and turn off the heat.

Cook the pasta in plenty of boiling water, drain and toss with the last 2 tablespoons of olive oil. Taste the pasta sauce. Season the pasta and then mix with the sauce. Toss in some rocket so that it just wilts (rather than gets all slimy) and serve in bowls with some grated Parmesan and plenty of black pepper.

123

white pizza

500 g strong white flour

7 g sachet dried yeast

150 ml warm water

1 tbsp clear honey

3 tbsp olive oil

Good pinch salt

Up to an additional 100 ml water

Extra olive oil

For the topping:

Approx. 200 g crème fraîche

1 small German salami, sliced or diced (approx. 50–100 g)

Few sprigs rosemary, oregano or thyme

100 g Gruyère, grated

Salt and pepper

Olive oil

This German dish consists of very thin dough that's rolled out to fit a rectangular shape and then topped with crème fraîche, some lardons, a little Gruyère and possibly some rosemary. German salami is equally nice, as are thyme and oregano. In fact, this lovely thin dough would work well with most toppings. Some sautéed mushrooms and taleggio would also be tasty and vegetarian. This makes 2 bases, which would feed 2 as light supper or one if you were feeling very greedy and kept nibbling on it all evening.

Serves 2–4

Mix all of the ingredients (except for the additional 100 ml water) together in a bowl with a dough paddle. You can add the extra 100 ml of water to make the dough come together, but add it slowly as you might not need it all. Also, be sure you get all the yeast in to the mixture – the dried stuff tends to settle at the bottom of the bowl when you mix it with warm water. Once the dough comes together, knead it for a minute and then place in a well-oiled bowl and cover with cling film. Leave to rise for about 3 hours until doubled in size.

Preheat your oven to its highest setting, or ideally, use a pizza stone! Divide the dough into 2 pieces and roll out as much as you can. It's quite elastic and will keep trying to shrink again. You can leave them on baking paper to prove and let them rise again for about 30 minutes. At this stage, roll it out a little more and then top with generous spoonfuls of the crème fraîche, a sprinkling of salami and herbs and scatter on the cheese. Then add plenty of black pepper, a small bit of salt and a good glug of olive oil.

Slide onto a baking tray or your pizza stone and bake until bubbling, golden brown and crisp. Cool slightly, slice and serve straightaway.

124

blonde lasagne

Good glug olive oil

1 large onion, peeled and diced

3 carrots, peeled and diced

1 head celery, finely sliced

Salt and pepper

8 cloves garlic, peeled and crushed

Some chopped herbs: thyme, oregano

300 g minced pork

300 g minced beef

¹/₂ bottle white wine

1 good tsp coriander seeds

Squeeze honey

Few splashes Worcestershire sauce

800 g tinned chopped tomatoes

6–8 lasagne sheets

For the béchamel sauce:

75 g butter

75 g flour

600 ml milk

1 good tbsp Dijon mustard

100 g Parmesan, grated

Grated nutmeg

This lasagne has all you'd expect from a typical lasagne, but it also uses of plenty of carrots, celery and fennel seeds to lighten up the flavours, as well as lots of white wine instead of red. It's also cooked more slowly. It ended up being a nice summery dish – a lighter, 'blonde' lasagne. The result is a really delicious dinner that you can stretch over two nights. It is delicious with a sharp green salad, good bread and a nice glass of white or red wine.

Serves 6–8 (and reheats well the next day)

Preheat the oven to 180°C. In a large, heavy-based saucepan, heat up the olive oil and sweat the onions, carrots and celery with the lid on so that you get a soft and vibrant mix as opposed to something that starts burning. Season well and then add in the garlic, herbs, pork and beef. You may have to stab at the clumps of meat to get them to separate and mix well. Once you feel you've broken up the mixture and both the veg and meat are well distributed, add the wine, turn the heat up and allow some liquid to evaporate as you will have an excess of liquid. Then add in the coriander, honey, Worcestershire sauce and tinned tomatoes. Stir well.

Put the lid on, turn the heat down and cook gently for 1 hour, giving it an occasional stir to make sure nothing is burning at the bottom. After an hour, remove the lid and cook until the excess liquid boils off and you have a nice-looking meat sauce. Taste and season well.

While this is going on, make your béchamel: melt the butter, add the flour and cook out for at least 1 minute using a wooden spoon to agitate and stir around the mixture in the pan. Add in the milk gradually, then change over to a whisk and whisk in the milk. Once it's all in there, reduce, stirring until it's thick but not gloopy, add the mustard and season well. Taste it and once you are happy, turn off the heat, add the Parmesan and some nutmeg and set aside until it's ready to assemble.

Spoon the meat mixture into a suitable gratin dish and then top with 6–8 sheets of lasagne. Pour the béchamel on top. You can bake this straight away for about 40 minutes (although you may have to cover the dish loosely with foil as the Parmesan can start to brown a little too much) and remove it at the end. Or you can let this cool completely and refrigerate overnight and cook from the fridge, although you may need to let it come to room temperature or cook for longer and at a slightly lower temperature, say 170°C, for 1 hour. Allow it to settle before slicing and serving.

orecchiette with squash, radicchio, walnuts and taleggio

1 butternut squash, peeled, seeded and diced

Approx. 100 ml olive oil

Salt and pepper

1 head radicchio, sliced

600 g taleggio, rind removed and cut into chunks

150 g walnuts, lightly toasted in the oven for 5 minutes

450 g orecchiette ('little ears')

For the béchamel:
50 g butter
50 g flour
450 ml milk
150 Gruyère, grated
50 g Parmesan, grated
Few sprigs rosemary
2 tbsp thyme leaves
Few grates nutmeg

This gorgeous dish is vegetarian, but be warned that that is no indication of its health merits, as it oozes rich Italian cheesiness. The roasted squash, radicchio and walnuts do temper this a little, as well as adding texture and depth to the béchamel-cloaked pasta.

This is the kind of dish to tuck into after walking in the hills, or climbing Mount Everest. Plonk yourself down in front of the fire with a bowlful and a glass of crisp, white wine.

Serves 6

Preheat the oven to 180°C. Roast the butternut squash on parchment paper with some olive oil and salt and pepper till tender. Meanwhile, cook the pasta in plenty of boiling water for 2–3 minutes. Drain, rinse and toss with a bit of olive oil to stop it sticking. Set aside.

To make the béchamel, melt the butter and add the flour. Cook out for at least 2–3 minutes to cook the flour, and then add the milk gradually and whisk continuously until the sauce comes together. Finally, add the herbs, grated cheese and nutmeg and stir till the cheese is melted. You can do this last bit off the heat.

To assemble, grease a deep baking dish with butter. Mix the pasta with the béchamel and put a layer of this mixture on the bottom of a deep baking dish Then add some squash, walnuts and radicchio, and scatter over half the taleggio. Then repeat.

Bake until melting and golden brown, about 30–40 minutes. You can also assemble and leave in your fridge until the next day and bake. If you do this, you may need to let it come up to room temperature or simply bake for longer. Cover with tinfoil if it browns too much on top.

126

spaghetti with aubergine and garlic breadcrumbs

3 good tbsp olive oil, at least

4 aubergines, finely diced

Salt and pepper

2 large onions, finely diced

8 cloves garlic, peeled and chopped

2 large tomatoes, roughly chopped

Thyme

800 g pasta

Zest of 1 lemon

For the breadcrumbs

3 tbsp olive oil

2 cloves garlic, peeled and crushed

1 tbsp oregano

120 g breadcrumbs

The aubergine ragu for this dish is delicious on its own. You could eat it as a condiment with some goat's cheese on toast and it would also be lovely with roast lamb. If you find caponata too strong, you will like the subtle meatiness of this dish, as there are no capers or red peppers to overpower the other flavours, just lots of aubergine and slow cooking, which produce a summer dish that suits chilly evenings. Don't feel obliged to make the breadcrumbs. They taste good, but are a hassle if you're strapped for time. This is based on a recipe by American-based French chef Laurent Tourondel.

Serves 6 (at least)

Heat the olive oil in a large non-stick saucepan and fry the aubergine on high heat in batches and season well. When it's all got colour, set aside and then sweat the onion until soft in more olive oil. You may need to use a big saucepan at this stage. Then simmer the aubergines, onions, garlic and tomatoes together, adding a cup of water to help bring it together. Season well, add the thyme and let it cook out for about 30 minutes. It will not look great, but once the water has cooked off and you let it cool down, you should taste great meaty flavours.

Cook the pasta in plenty of boiling water, drain, toss with some olive oil, season and add some lemon zest. Mix with the sauce and serve with the breadcrumbs on top.

Mix all the ingredients together and then bake for 15 or 20 minutes at 150°C until getting brown and toasted. You'll have to mix occasionally and may need to cook it for longer, but just make sure it's golden brown.

lazy lasagne

Good glug olive oil

2 onions, peeled and chopped

6 cloves garlic, peeled and sliced

Salt and pepper

500 g mushrooms, roughly chopped

1200 g tinned chopped tomatoes

2 aubergines, diced

1 good tbsp tomato purée

Dried oregano

10–12 lasagne sheets (no-pre-cook kind)

Approx. 200 g crème fraîche

250 g cheddar, grated

A good old-fashioned lasagne is an incredibly satisfying thing to eat, but it can often seem far too indulgent to make the long-winded meat and cheesy version. This is a lazy and vegetarian way of rustling up a lasagne, from start to finish in just over an hour. It's light enough on the calories and one that you'll probably be able to get children and non-dieters to eat without moaning. It's also one of those dinners that you can get two nights out of, which always makes me happy. Coming home in the depths of winter and knowing that dinner just needs to be reheated is a nice feeling.

Serves 8

Preheat the oven to 190°C. In a large saucepan, sweat the onions in the olive oil until soft and add in the garlic. Season well and then throw in the mushrooms and tomatoes. Together they produce quite a lot of water, so when the mixture is bubbling away and very liquidy, chuck in the aubergines, which will soak up all that excess liquid. Cook out for about 10 minutes, check the seasoning and add in some tomato purée and herbs at this stage.

In a good-sized gratin dish, add one layer of tomato mixture, then a layer of the lasagne sheets, breaking them to fit, then more tomato, then another layer of sheets and finish up with a very thin layer of tomato sauce on the top.

Then sprinkle the cheddar on top and dot the crème fraîche in blobs evenly on top of the cheese. Bake at 190°C for 45 minutes until bubbling and golden brown.

roast cauliflower spaghetti

1 head cauliflower

4 tbsp olive oil

Salt and pepper

Grate nutmeg or pinch chilli flakes

A couple of knobs butter

3 cloves garlic, peeled and crushed

Splash white wine

Basil leaves

250–300 g wholewheat spaghetti

50 g hazelnuts, lightly toasted

A scrape of hard goat's cheese or Pecorino to garnish (optional)

Roasting cauliflower is simple and produces a super tasty and healthy snack or starter. Just chop florets into small pieces, scatter some olive oil, salt, pepper and whatever spices you fancy over them and then blast in the oven until charred and slightly tender. You can flavour it using spices such as turmeric, mild curry powder or chilli flakes. Also don't shy away from the green leaves on the cauliflower; chop these up and throw them in. The ideal time is 20 minutes or so in a hot oven (approx. 200°C), but you may have to shake the pan and change the oven temperature if necessary.

Serves 4

Preheat the oven to 200°C. You can toast your hazelnuts while your oven is preheating, but do keep an eye on them. They won't take kindly to full-blown temp of 200°C, so catch the oven on the way up.

Cut the cauliflower into florets, give them a little rinse and shake off the water (you don't want them steaming). Put them into a roasting tin, sprinkle with half the olive oil and season with salt, pepper, nutmeg or chilli. Roast them for 20–30 minutes. You want a little char and a little crunch. Don't fret about turning your oven up full blast and tweaking cooking times.

Meanwhile, heat up your butter and add the garlic. Then add the white wine and roughly chopped basil. Season and set aside.

Cook your spaghetti in a large pot of boiling water, drain, then add the rest of the olive oil while draining and mix it with a pasta spoon or tongs so the oil coats the spaghetti. Season with some salt and pepper. Put it back in the big saucepan and add the butter sauce and roasted cauliflower and toss. Spoon into bowls and top with the hazelnuts and some grated cheese.

129

butternut squash, mushroom and taleggio lasagne

2 butternut squash, peeled, diced and seeds removed

Olive oil

Salt and pepper

1 kg button mushrooms, sliced

4 cloves garlic, peeled and crushed

400 g taleggio, roughly cubed

400 g tinned chopped tomatoes

1 tbsp miso paste

3–4 lasagne sheets

Chopped parsley to serve

This is a very simple dish as it will mostly cook away in the oven, and the mushroom and tomato mixture will just quietly simmer on the stove until it's nice and dry. With that big whack of miso paste in there, you get a meatiness that's still vegetarian. There is a lot of taleggio in this, but when you sink your fork into a spoonful of it and hit a molten seam of golden, oozing cheese, you won't regret it. Feel free to substitute goat's cheese or anything else you fancy.

Serves 6–8

Preheat the oven to 190°C. Season the diced squash generously with olive oil and salt and pepper and bake on a parchment-covered roasting tray for 20–30 minutes until tender. Then lower the oven to 180°C.

Meanwhile, over a medium heat, sauté the sliced mushrooms in the olive oil with the garlic, taking care not to burn the garlic. It'll start off looking like a huge amount of mushrooms, but after 5 or 10 minutes, they will have shrunk considerably and the whole mixture will have wilted down. Add in the tomatoes and the miso and cook out for about 10–15 minutes until quite dry.

To assemble the lasagne, place the soft squash at the bottom of the dish and then dot half the taleggio around it. Place the lasagne sheets on top, and then add all of the mushroom mix on top of that. Finally, dot the remaining taleggio all over the top and bake for 30–40 minutes.

SIDES

130

asparagus with miso butter

100 g miso paste
200 g butter
Splash sherry vinegar
2 bunches asparagus, bases trimmed
Olive oil
Salt

Miso is a Japanese paste that's usually made from fermented soybeans and is hugely tasty but has lots of salt. There are those who say it also has plenty of health benefits as long as you don't cook it too much. It's a big part of the Japanese diet and is utterly delicious, so I guess all that's required is a little moderation. It goes really well with asparagus.

Serves 4 as a side

First make the butter by mixing it in a food processor with the miso and the vinegar. Wrap it in cling film and roll up into a sausage shape. That way you can freeze it and cut slices from it to use at your leisure.

You can cook the asparagus two ways. You can take the trimmed stems and rub in a little olive oil and season with salt. Heat up your chargrill pan till really hot and chargrill them till nicely charred on all sides. Then add in a good chunk of the miso butter, let it sizzle and then put the asparagus onto a large platter and let everyone dig in.

Alternatively, you can put the asparagus in a small roasting tray with a good slice of the miso butter and let them roast in the oven at about 220°C for 6–8 minutes until starting to char nicely.

131

chargrilled broccoli with lemon, chilli and garlic

2 heads broccoli

100 ml olive oil

6 cloves garlic, peeled and thinly sliced

2 red chillies, deseeded and thinly sliced

Salt and pepper

Juice of 1 lemon

You can't really go wrong with these four ingredients: broccoli, lemon, chilli and garlic. How could they not work well together?

Serves 4–6 as a side

Separate the broccoli into little florets. Have a colander ready in your sink. Bring a large pot of water to the boil and cook the broccoli for just 1 minute. Drain and rinse in plenty of cold water until the florets are genuinely cold. Drain well and put in the fridge to chill thoroughly and dry off further.

Meanwhile, heat half the olive oil in a small saucepan with the garlic and chillies. Cook very gently for a few minutes until the garlic is soft and set aside. When the broccoli is dry, toss in a bowl with the remaining olive oil and plenty of salt and pepper.

Heat up a chargrill or heavy-based frying pan until smoking and chargrill the broccoli in batches until nicely charred in parts. Put them back into a large mixing bowl and when they're all done, toss with the lemon juice and chilli and garlic oil. This tastes great when served warm or at room temperature, but doesn't last too long in the fridge!

132

chickpea and coriander salad

2 red onions, peeled and very finely sliced

5 garlic cloves, peeled and very finely sliced

200 ml olive oil, approx.

2 red chillies, seeded and finely chopped

Salt and pepper

800 g tinned chickpeas, drained and rinsed

Bunch spring onions, finely chopped

Bunch coriander, parsley, mint or basil (about 50 g in total)

Juice of 1 lemon

250 g feta or goat's cheese, roughly chopped

Serves 4–6 as a side

Heat half the olive oil and sweat the red onions and garlic for about 5 minutes until soft, then add the red chillies. Allow to cool. Season this oil very well with salt and pepper.

In a large bowl, mix the onion and oil mixture with the chickpeas, spring onions and herbs. Add the lemon juice, mix well and season. Add some more of the remaining 100 ml of olive oil if you want to make it more luscious and then add the cheese and mix carefully. Check the seasoning again and serve.

crushed spuds with watercress and horseradish

1 kg new or small potatoes

30 g fresh horseradish, finely grated

250 g Greek yoghurt

Few tbsp crème fraîche (if you have it)

50 g watercress, roughly torn

Salt and pepper

This dish was sort of made up as it happened. Watercress, fresh horseradish and a load of Greek yoghurt all get jumbled together with some leftover potatoes and the result is just delicious, particularly when served warm.

Serves 4–6 as a side

Boil the potatoes in plenty of salted water until just tender. Mix the horseradish and yoghurt together. Drain the potatoes and dump them in a large bowl. Then do a really poor job at mashing them so that they are just crushed.

Mix together the yoghurt and the crème fraîche and add to the potatoes and the watercress and season well. Serve warm.

134

carrot salad with ginger and lemon

1 kg carrots

1 red onion, peeled and very thinly diced

Juice of 2 lemons

150 ml olive oil

Salt

Lots of black pepper

1 tsp honey

1 tsp Dijon mustard

3½-inch piece ginger, peeled and finely grated

½ tsp ground cardamom

Cardamom is a member of the ginger family and you can buy it dried and ready to go or else encased in little green pods that are squidgy and delicious, especially with chocolate and coffee flavours. The carrot salad here is a great example of simple flavours but when you take the time to mix them properly, you get the full impact of sweet and sharp.

Serves at least 6 as a side

Peel the carrots and then grate them in a food processor (if possible). Put into a large bowl and then add the onions.

Shake the ingredients for the dressing in a little jar or whisk them together: lemon juice, olive oil, salt, pepper, honey, mustard, ginger and cardamom. Add this to the carrots and mix well. Season and taste. Feel free to add spring onions or chopped herbs.

(See Lamb two ways for photo, p. 96.)

braised baby gem

4 heads baby gem

Approx. 50 g butter

Good splash olive oil

Approx. 100 ml water

Few sprigs thyme

2 cloves garlic, peeled and crushed

Salt and pepper

Cooked lettuce? It might seem a little out there, but give it a go. It's a really tasty side dish that even children will like and it only takes a few minutes to cook.

Serves 4 as a side

Slice the baby gems in half lengthways. If some outer leaves fall off, so be it: don't bother cooking them. Heat the butter and olive oil until foaming and fry the baby gem flat side down for about a minute or until just starting to colour in parts. Add about 100 ml water, the thyme and garlic and then season very well.

Cook on a high heat for about another minute, baste the lettuces or turn them over gently and serve with a small bit of the garlicky, buttery cooking liquid.

white bean and mushroom gratin

1 onion, peeled and finely chopped

30 g butter

Splash white wine

150 ml cream

2–4 cloves garlic, peeled and sliced

400 g mushrooms (any variety you fancy)

Salt and pepper

400 g tinned haricot/cannellini beans

Bit of parsley, chopped

Lemon juice

Bit of grated Parmesan or other hard cheese

Mushrooms are one of those vegetables that you should never feel guilty about buying in the winter (unlike red peppers and asparagus). They are cheap and nutritious and suit hearty dishes. This white bean and mushroom gratin is a great example of what you can do cheaply and quickly for a no-meat, no-fuss meal. It's good for you, even though there's a bit of cream, and it makes a very satisfying meal.

Serves 4 as a side, 2 as a main course

Fry the onion in half the butter until golden brown. Add the wine, cream and garlic. Turn up the heat and simmer until the mixture has reduced slightly. This should only take about 5 minutes of stirring and simmering in total.

Meanwhile, fry the mushrooms in the rest of the butter over a high heat and add even more garlic if you fancy. Season the mushrooms well. Try and get some good colour on the mushrooms as this will help them take on more flavour. Add the cream infusion.

Drain and rinse the beans with water from a boiled kettle. When well drained, add to the mushrooms. Mix well, heat thoroughly, check the seasoning and add the parsley and the lemon juice if you need to sharpen it up. Plenty of black pepper would also work.

Pour into a gratin dish, grate some Parmesan over the top and grill for a few minutes until golden brown. Serve with some crusty bread and a bit of salad.

137

roast parsnips and carrots with fennel, honey and seeds

1 kg carrots, peeled and cut into wedges

1 kg parsnips, peeled and cut into wedges

4 tbsp olive oil

Salt and pepper

2 tbsp honey

4 tsp fennel seeds

Splash water

To serve:

2 tbsp mixed seeds

These parsnips and carrots are done in just a slick of olive oil and liberally sprinkled with seeds to add crunch and a hint of spice and would go well with any roast meat.

Serves 8 as a side

Preheat the oven to 200°C. Toss the wedges of carrot and parsnip in the olive oil, season well and put in a roasting tin, ensuring there's plenty of space around them to allow the air to circulate as they roast.

Cook for 15 minutes, then take out and add the honey and the fennel seeds plus a splash of water to stop the whole thing burning. Return to the oven and cook for another 15–20 minutes or until tender and starting to brown. To serve, toss with the seeds.

138

purple sprouting broccoli with lemon and hazelnuts

50 g butter
1 tbsp hazelnuts, chopped
Juice and zest of 1 lemon
Salt and pepper
250 g purple sprouting broccoli

This is lovely, simple dish with a perfect lemony, nutty, buttery balance. It would even work as a snack or as a casual starter.

Serves 2 as a side

Melt the butter over a gentle heat, add the hazelnuts, turn up the heat and when they're just starting to brown, add the lemon zest and juice and season well. Beware of splashes of hot fat. Keep warm. Trim any stalky bits off the broccoli. Blanch in boiling water for a minute, drain and serve immediately with the hazelnut butter spooned over.

avocado and roast beetroot salad with blood orange

4 fresh beetroot

Salt and pepper

Juice 1 lemon

Handful fresh tarragon, chopped

2 avocadoes (just ripe), sliced

1 blood orange, peeled and segmented

Olive oil

This salad is a play on the classic beetroot/citrus combination. Beetroot, if you like its warm earthiness, is a true superfood, packed with energy-giving vitamins and other nutrients.

Serves 4–6 as a side

Preheat the oven to 160°C. Peel the beetroot, wrap each one in tinfoil and roast in the oven till tender, which should take about 45–50 minutes. Remove from foil and slice into segments as you would an apple.

From here, it's all assembly. Gently toss the ingredients together in the lemon juice, herbs and olive oil and season well. This is a fresh, robust salad.

140

shredded sprouts with truffle oil

By shredding Brussels sprouts in a food processor and slowly sautéing them in some simmering, buttery water along with some chilli flakes and a few drops of truffle oil, you can create a great dish that even non-sprout-lovers might like. This would be lovely with roast chicken or grilled pork chops or even on its own.

Serves 4–6 as a side

600 g Brussels sprouts, shredded/grated in a food mixer
50 g butter
250 ml vegetable stock or water
Few chilli flakes
Salt and pepper
Few glugs olive oil
Few splashes truffle oil

Melt the butter and add the stock or water and chilli flakes. When simmering, add the grated sprouts and, keeping the heat up, cook until tasty and just soft. The sprouts just seem to absorb all the stock and cook just enough to retain all their flavour. Be sure to allow any excess liquid to evaporate – keep the lid off and add the olive and truffle oils when the mixture is 'dry', adjusting it to suit your tastes. Then serve. They should take less than 5 minutes to cook.

141

broccoli salad with avocado and chilli dressing

1 head broccoli, cut into florets

200 g frozen peas

Approx. 100 g mixed baby leaves (spinach, mesclun, etc.)

400 g tinned chickpeas, drained and rinsed

4 tbsp mixed seeds (linseed, pumpkin, sunflower, etc.)

100 g flaked almonds

100 g feta or firm goat's cheese

Small bunch spring onions, finely chopped

Sprouted beans to garnish

For the dressing:

1 green chilli

1 very ripe avocado

75 ml Greek yoghurt

Bunch mint

Juice of 1 lime

Olive oil

Salt and pepper

This broccoli recipe is the perfect winter salad: filling, tasty, nutritious and, with its creamy avocado dressing, a little bit luxurious. The mint adds zing, while the chickpeas and toasted almonds add crunch and flavour. This is lovely on its own, but try it with leftover shoulder of lamb. They complement each other very nicely.

Serves 4 as a side, 2–3 as a main course

Blanch the broccoli for 1 minute in boiling water, and then 'refresh' to stop it cooking by running it under cold water until it's cooled down. Do the same with the peas, boiling them for just about 30 seconds before refreshing. Drain them both really well so you're not making a salad out of waterlogged vegetables.

Toast the almonds in the oven or in a frying pan over a medium heat. Crumble the feta, and then toss all the ingredients together to assemble the salad.

To make the dressing, place the ingredients in a blender and whizz till smooth. Season well. To serve, spoon some salad onto plates and add a dollop of the creamy dressing and, for added goodness, a few sprouted beans.

142

baked onions

6 large Spanish onions

100 g butter

150–200 g breadcrumbs

Small bunch parsley

1 clove garlic, peeled and
crushed

250 ml cream

Small bunch sage, chopped

100 g Parmesan or cheddar
(or mix of the two)

Generous pinch grated nutmeg

Salt and pepper

Everyone loves these guys: full of sweet onion flavour, they are delicious on their own or served with roast meat instead of spuds.

Serves 6 as a side

Preheat the oven to 200°C. Trim the root of the onions and, keeping the skin on, make an incision in each onion three-quarters of the way up near the top. With the root side down, wrap each onion in tinfoil, place in a roasting tin half-filled with water and bake in the oven until very tender, for about 1 hour. Reduce the oven to 170°C.

When the onions are soft, remove the tops, cutting along the incision line, and scoop out the soft flesh inside, which you then chop or blitz quickly in a food processor (don't make mush of it though; a quick pulse should do it).

Heat the butter in a large pan and, to make the stuffing, add the flesh of the onions, the breadcrumbs, parsley, garlic, cream, sage and half the cheese. Season with nutmeg, salt and pepper. Finally, top each onion with a generous cap of grated cheese and bake for 20 minutes until golden brown and bubbling.

143

quinoa salad

Approx. 200 g quinoa

Few tbsp olive oil

Black sesame seeds or nigella seeds

Bunch coriander, finely chopped

Salt and pepper

4 preserved lemons, finely chopped, or juice and zest of 1–2 lemons

Quinoa is great thrown into most salads when you want the bit of texture that you can get from nuts but without all the calories.

Serves approx. 4 as a side

Cook the quinoa in boiling water for about 9 minutes and then drain and rinse until cold. Let it drain really well – otherwise it will be too soggy. Simply toss with the rest of the ingredients and season to taste.

144

pomegranate and green bean salad

450 g green beans

1 red onion, peeled and thinly sliced

1 pomegranate

Small bunch flat-leaf parsley, chopped

Small bunch chopped mint, chopped

Dressing:

1 tsp Dijon mustard

1 clove garlic, peeled and chopped

50 ml white wine vinegar

150 ml olive oil

2 tbsp honey

Salt and pepper

Serves 4 as a side

Blanch the beans, scoop out the pomegranate seeds, make the dressing – simply by putting the ingredients in a jar and shaking – and toss the whole lot together.

buttermilk and kale mash

Approx. 1.3 kg potatoes

1 big bunch kale, more if you are a fan

80 ml olive oil

3 cloves garlic, peeled and crushed

350 ml buttermilk

1–2 tbsp horseradish sauce

Salt and pepper

120 g goat's cheese or 50 g Parmesan shavings (optional)

This mash would happily go with anything you can think of, as it is so lovely, green, satisfying and tangy (without oodles of butter and cream). It would also be an ideal supper to have with just a fried or poached egg perched on top. Leave the goat's cheese off this recipe if serving it with beef and use a little Parmesan or pecorino on top instead. The quantity of spuds is quite large, but you could make it and serve it with stew on night one and then as a vegetarian version on night two, with the aforementioned egg on top, or just a few blobs of goat's cheese and some wilted spinach.

Serves 6–8 as a side

Bring the potatoes to boil in a large saucepan and cook until tender. Remove and discard the heavy stalks from the kale and roughly chop the leaves. Heat the olive oil in a saucepan and add the kale plus a good splash of water from kettle and put a lid on it. Let the heat shrink the kale down into something a lot more manageable, then remove the lid and cook so that it dries out a bit and then add the garlic.

Turn off the heat, drain the potatoes and put them back in their saucepan and let the residual heat of your cooker help dry out the spuds. Then mash the potatoes with their skins and stir in the buttermilk and cooked kale.

Mix well, adding the horseradish sauce and season to taste. This can be reheated with a little water or extra buttermilk as it will dry out and it's easier to heat up if it's a bit 'looser'. Serve with the goat's cheese if you're making it into a stand-alone supper or Parmesan if you're eating it with beef.

(See Tile-makers' stew for photo, p. 70.)

baked potatoes with crisp kale, bacon and crème fraîche with verjus

4 large potatoes
6 streaky rashers
100 ml verjus
200–250 g crème fraîche
Approx. 300 g curly kale
1–2 tbsp olive oil
1 tsp maple syrup or honey
Salt and pepper

This recipe contains all the things that go best with spuds: curly kale, bacon, crème fraîche and verjus. Delicious. If you can't get verjus, then use the juice from one lemon.

Serves 4 as a side

Preheat the oven to 200°C. Make a slice horizontally around the well-washed potatoes. Bake them for the guts of an hour. They should be a lovely dark brown, with very crisp skins and soft flesh.

In the interim, grill the rashers until very crisp with hardly any fat left on them. Blot dry with paper towel. Then cool and then blend on pulse mode in a food processor until they resemble 'bacon bits'. You can also do this by chopping them very finely by hand.

Reduce the verjus in small saucepan until it's about 1 tablespoon's worth. (If you are using lemon juice, don't bother reducing!) Cool down and mix with the crème fraîche along with the maple syrup and lots of black pepper.

Prep your curly kale by washing it well, then removing and discarding the stalks. Rinse and then toss with the olive oil and some salt. Bake at about 150°C and after about 5 minutes, move the bits about as some will be starting to burn. It burns very quickly, but you do want it to be crisp.

Cook this while you scoop out the flesh of the potatoes and mash lightly with the crème fraîche, along with the maple syrup. Don't overwork the spuds or be tempted to put them in a food processor – you'll excite all the starch and will be left with gluey spuds, rather than light and delicious potato magic. Taste and season, and stuff the mash back into the potato skins. Keep checking the kale and when it's cooked and crisp, serve with the spuds and topping.

balsamic potatoes

1.3 kg large potatoes

150 ml olive oil

3 cloves garlic, peeled and crushed

Salt and pepper

150 ml balsamic vinegar

Rosemary

The spuds are really delicious and would go fantastically well with the rich flavours of venison. They are also nice to eat even if they are not piping hot, which can be a challenge if plating up for a big crowd.

Serves 8 or more as a side

You'll probably need to do this in two batches. Slice each potato in half (vertically) and then cut each half into wedges. Fry the potatoes in a non-stick frying pan (you'll need a lid for it) in a half or a third of the olive oil, depending on how many batches you're doing.

Once the potatoes have started to brown, add the appropriate amount of garlic, salt, pepper and balsamic vinegar as well as some rosemary. Cover with the lid and cook until the potatoes are tender. Then remove the lid and cook on high to crisp up the potatoes and let any residual liquid evaporate. They should be a really dark colour, tender and very tasty. You can transfer them to a serving dish and, if necessary, give them a blast in the oven before serving.

148

rhubarb and lentil salad

200 g Puy lentils
50 ml olive oil
Salt and pepper
2 corn on the cob
6–8 rhubarb stalks
1 bunch asparagus
1 bunch spring onions
Big bunch flat-leaf parsley
200 g halloumi
Another splash olive oil
Splash balsamic or lime juice

Using 'raw' rhubarb in salads is great. It's best described as a kind of 'juicy' celery and really adds an interesting crunch to most salads. It's also a good way of making Puy lentils into something a bit more summery.

Serves 6–8 as a side

Cook the Puy lentils in boiling water until tender and then drain and give them a quick rinse with cold water. Drain them really well and then mix with the 50 ml olive oil and season well. You can cook the corn on a chargrill briefly to give it some flavour – just rub it with some olive oil, salt and pepper and char on all sides – or else cook for a few minutes in boiling water, drain and cut the corn from the cob and add to the salad. Chop up the rhubarb and add it in.

Either chargrill the asparagus or quickly blanch or steam them, then refresh in cold water and add to the lentils. Add in the spring onions, and chop up the flat-leaf parsley.

Chop the halloumi into cubes, fry in olive oil until golden brown and then drain on kitchen paper. Add the halloumi, taste and adjust the seasoning.

This salad is fine after a night in the fridge, but I prefer to make it fresh and then, while all the veg are still a little warm, serve straight away. Sharpen up with the vinegar or lime juice if necessary.

chargrilled asparagus with marinated courgette and halloumi

Approx. 300 g cherry tomatoes, halved

Sprinkle caster sugar

Salt and pepper

24 asparagus spears

Approx. 150 ml olive oil

200 g halloumi

2 courgettes

Lemon juice

Bunch rocket

400 g mixed leaves

Basil leaves

For the vinaigrette:

1 tsp Dijon mustard

2 tbsp sherry vinegar

100 ml olive oil

Salt and pepper

This asparagus salad with courgette and grilled halloumi is a great party dish. Obviously try to do it when asparagus is in season and plentiful.

Serves 4–6 as a side

Preheat the oven to 140°C. Cover a baking tray in parchment paper, and put the cherry tomatoes on it skin-side down and sprinkle with a tiny bit of caster sugar and salt. You can also sprinkle with some dried herbs for extra flavour. Roast for about an hour, then set aside until ready to assemble. These need to stay out at room temperature.

Trim the asparagus and then toss in a bowl with a good lick of olive oil and some salt and pepper. Heat up a griddle or chargrill pan, and when really hot, put the asparagus on top in a neat row. Turn them from side to side so they get evenly charred. After a few minutes, they should be nicely charred and still have lots of bite. Take the off the heat and set aside.

While the griddle is still hot, chargrill slices of the halloumi till nice and brown on each side and then also set aside and keep at room temperature.

Toss the ingredients together for the dressing so it's ready to go later. Cut the courgettes into thin ribbons with a vegetable peeler or mandolin. Then toss with some olive oil, salt and lemon juice, which will lightly 'cook' it. When you want to serve, just assemble by tossing the mixed leaves and rocket with some vinaigrette. Then lay out the chargrilled asparagus, halloumi and drape the courgette over. Top with basil leaves and the roast tomatoes and serve.

150

warm tomato salad

4 slices sourdough bread

200 ml olive oil

6 cloves garlic, peeled and crushed

1 red onion, peeled and finely sliced

Salt and pepper

3 tbsp red wine vinegar

1 tbsp capers

1 kg tomatoes (whole cherry and chopped plum tomatoes)

1 bunch basil, chopped

1 big bunch chives, chopped

Handful Parmesan, finely grated

Some dishes, whether warm or hot, are absolutely great in the summertime. This warm tomato salad is one such dish, its only downside being that it has to be consumed as soon as you've made it.

Serves 4 as a side

Break the bread into big bite-sized chunks and bake in a moderate oven for 5–10 minutes until golden brown and crisp. Leave to cool. You could do this the night before. If you don't have time, you could simply toast the bread well and break into chunks.

You can do this next bit well in advance if you want: very gently heat up the olive oil and garlic. No colour, just warm through. Then add the red onion and stir. Turn off the heat and leave to soften in the warm oil. Season well and set aside until you are ready to eat, as it won't take long to finish.

Chop the larger tomatoes into quarters if you are using different types: basically have them all a similar size but use whatever combination you like. You can use some whole cherry tomatoes, some quartered plum tomatoes and a few roughly chopped larger ones.

When you are ready to do the final blast of cooking, heat up the olive oil with the garlic and onions and get very warm. Add in the vinegar and capers and try to get the mixture hot and bubbling. Then add in the tomatoes and stir for a minute. Turn off the heat and add in the bread, the herbs and the Parmesan. Stir in some more black pepper and then dole out into bowls and serve straight away.

151

giant couscous salad

1 large onion, peeled and diced

Splash olive oil

400 g giant couscous

Salt and pepper

Very large mixed bunch parsley, coriander, basil

2–3 pomegranates

For the dressing:

100 ml olive oil

50 ml sherry vinegar

3 tsp Dijon mustard

Good squeeze honey

2 cloves garlic, peeled and crushed

Salt and pepper

Giant couscous is a great starchy salad that is well worth trying. It seems to hold up to strong flavours and doesn't suck all the flavours out of everything around it.

In a large heavy-based saucepan, sweat the onion in the olive oil until soft but not coloured. Add the couscous and mix well so that the grains get coated and take on a bit of flavour. Season them well. Add plenty of boiling water, bring to the boil and then cook for about 10 minutes. (Check the instructions on the pack, but it's usually 10–12 minutes.) Drain the couscous well. Then tip into a large bowl and mix lightly with a fork.

Mix the ingredients for the dressing together and pour onto the couscous. Season very well. If leaving it as a salad, let it cool down and then add in the pomegranate juice and seeds, which will sweeten and cool it down further. Taste and then add in the chopped herbs. You can adjust the seasoning further by adding some lemon juice, more sherry vinegar or even red wine vinegar. This salad is best served at room temperature.

(See Crisp shredded lamb for photo, p. 103)

152

lavash

290 g plain flour
200 g cooked quinoa
1 tsp poppy seeds
3 tsp fennel seeds
Good pinch salt
Good pinch sugar
330 ml milk
50 g melted butter
Olive oil
Few pinches sumac or extra seeds

Even if you are terrible at baking breads and fear attempting it, this lavash flatbread is great fun to make and the results are sublimely professional. The recipe calls for the lovely Middle Eastern spice, sumac, but if you can't find it, some poppy seeds and rock salt are fine.

Mix all the ingredients together (except for the olive oil and sumac/extra seeds) in a food processor. It will form a very wet dough. Chill for at least 20 minutes or overnight. Preheat the oven to 180°C.

Line a few baking trays with parchment paper. Take a handful of the wet dough and smear on the paper as through you were trying to form a very thin, even layer of plaster on the parchment. It should be nearly see-through. Do this on each sheet (you may get 4–6 sheets out of it) and then sprinkle with sumac or extra seeds and a little drizzle of olive oil.

Bake until crisp and golden brown. Cut or break into big pieces and serve.

153

strawberry and goat's cheese salad

1 cucumber

2 punnets strawberries, hulled

2 good tbsp olive oil

Juice of 1 lemon

Good squeeze honey or maple syrup

100 g soft goat's cheese, crumbled

1 small red onion

Big bunch basil

Black pepper

For the balsamic syrup:

200 ml balsamic vinegar

Sprig rosemary

Good squeeze honey or maple syrup

2 tbsp olive oil

If you can find some delicious Irish strawberries, try this dish immediately. It manages to combine fruit and cheese into one sublime course, thus eliminating a cheese course and dessert so you get the best of both worlds.

Serves 4–6 as a side

First, make the balsamic syrup: heat up the balsamic vinegar and the sprig of rosemary very gently until simmering. You really need to keep an eye on it. Reduce it down by a third and then remove from the heat, discard the rosemary and whisk in the honey or maple syrup and olive oil. Be warned: once it starts to reduce, it's a slippery slope to becoming burnt, so take it handy with the heat.

Peel the cucumber and then cut in half lengthways. Using a teaspoon, scoop out the seeds. Then cut the cucumber into thin slices so you get half moons. Cut the strawberries in half and gently toss in the olive oil, lemon juice and honey or maple syrup. Do this in the bowl you will serve it in. Then scatter the cucumber around the dish. Add the goat's cheese and a sprinkling of onion and basil. Give a light mix and then drizzle with your balsamic syrup and serve.

This will go mushy quite quickly, so assemble close to serving time, although you can have some of the prep done. You can certainly hull the strawberries, prep the cucumber and have the balsamic syrup ready – just don't toss the strawberries with the olive oil and lemon juice until the last minute.

154

tomato barley risotto

200 g pearl barley

30 g butter

90 ml olive oil

1 head celery, finely sliced

1 large onion, peeled and finely diced

4 garlic cloves, peeled and sliced

Few sprigs thyme

Pinch smoked paprika

1 bay leaf

4 strips lemon rind

Good pinch chilli flakes, (optional)

400 g tinned tomatoes

700 ml vegetable stock

300 ml passata

Salt and pepper

For the garnish (optional):

Fresh oregano or other herbs

Caraway seeds (optional)

100 g crumbled feta (optional)

Extra olive oil

Grated Parmesan (optional)

This tomato barley risotto is another recipe adapted from Yotam Ottolenghi. It's a very tasty dish and one the children also wolf down without a peep. It is full of celery, garlic, tomatoes and a hint of smoked paprika, topped with anything from crumbled feta to a little bit of Parmesan. Not only is pearl barley great for you, it is also cheap and you don't have to stand over this while it's cooking. You just have to stir frequently, but not constantly.

Serves 4 as a side

Rinse the barley really well and drain while you melt the butter and olive oil in a heavy-based saucepan. Add the celery, onions, garlic and thyme and sweat until they are soft. Then add the drained barley and mix well. Then add in the rest of the ingredients and stir well.

Bring up to the boil and then gently simmer for about 45 minutes, stirring frequently rather than constantly. The barley should have soaked up the liquid and should be the consistency of a risotto. If not, keep cooking until the liquid has pretty much all gone, but it's wet enough to not turn into complete stodge.

The garnish is optional, but nice: lightly toast some caraway seeds in a frying pan and mix with crumbled feta and some olive oil and spoon over. A bit of grated Parmesan is probably the best option for kids.

155

garlic roasted new potato salad

500 g small new potatoes

2 tbsp olive oil

1 tbsp chopped rosemary

1 tbsp chopped oregano or
thyme

4 cloves garlic, peeled and very
finely sliced

Salt and pepper

2–3 good tbsp crème fraîche

1 tbsp cider vinegar

Big bunch flat-leaf parsley,
roughly chopped

Juice of 1 lemon

Pinch sugar

Serves 4–6 as a side

Preheat the oven to 200°C. Cut the potatoes in half. Toss with the herbs, garlic and plenty of salt and pepper and roast for about 45 minutes. Keep an eye on the garlic, and if you think it's going to start burning, cover with tinfoil for the first half of the cooking time.

Mix together the crème fraîche, cider vinegar, parsley and lemon juice. Season well with the sugar, salt and plenty of black pepper. Let the potatoes cool down and then mix with the crème fraîche dressing. Be careful not to break them up. Taste and season as necessary. This salad is fine to make the day before.

156

summer crunchy caprese

1 ball buffalo mozzarella
1 head fennel, sliced
1 head celery, sliced
400 g tinned borlotti beans, rinsed and drained
2 heads cos lettuce

For the dressing:
1 tbsp wholegrain mustard
2 cloves garlic, peeled and crushed
1 tbsp honey or agave syrup
6 tbsp olive oil
3 tbsp balsamic vinegar
Good pinch turmeric
A little grated ginger
Salt and pepper

Simplest is generally best for a great caprese, but if you are looking for something a bit more adventurous, this dish fits the bill. The strong dressing does undoubtedly affect the delicate flavour of the mozzarella, but the joy of mozzarella is also in the texture and it works really well in this salad.

Serves 4 as a side, 2 as a main course

Make the dressing by mixing the mustard, garlic and honey and then whisking in the olive oil very slowly. Then whisk in the vinegar, ginger and turmeric. Set aside.

Tear up the mozzarella and mix with the fennel, celery and beans. Toss in the dressing, add the lettuce, mix well and serve.

157

paprika and onion roast potatoes

600 g small potatoes
2 onions, peeled and quartered
1 tsp hot paprika
1 tsp smoked paprika
Salt and pepper
2 tbsp olive oil

An easy potato dish that doesn't require too much expertise or effort, but which still tastes great.

Serves 6 as a side

Preheat the oven to 180°C. Chop the potatoes into big bite-sized chunks and toss with the rest of the ingredients making sure everything is well coated. Roast for about 30 minutes until golden brown and tender. If the spuds need longer, turn down the oven to 160°C and cook for another 15 minutes.

158

fried aubergines with mint and vinegar

4 tbsp breadcrumbs

100 ml olive oil

2 cloves garlic, peeled and crushed

Salt and black pepper

2 aubergines, sliced 2 cm thick

3 tbsp red wine vinegar

1 tsp caster sugar

Pinch chilli flakes

Small bunch mint

These aubergines, which are adapted from a recipe in the Bocca Cookbook, *go really well with meatballs, multi-tasking their way onto the plate by being both a lightly pickled salad as well as a sharp, savoury condiment. They would also be lovely served on a big platter for a casual barbecue accompaniment as they are best served at room temperature.*

Serves 4 as a side

Preheat the oven to 160°C. Mix the breadcrumbs with about 40 ml of the olive oil, the garlic, some salt and pepper. (You can always add some dried herbs such as oregano to this or chopped fresh herbs, like thyme and rosemary.) Spread the breadcrumbs onto a shallow dish and bake until golden brown. You may need to scatter and shake them occasionally as they cook from the outside in. When they look golden and crunchy, set aside to cool. They are fine to sit out for a few hours.

Using another 40 ml of olive oil, heat a large non-stick frying pan with a little oil and fry the slices of aubergine in batches until golden brown on both sides. You really need to season them well, as they just absorb salt and oil – but they will taste fabulous.

Lay them out on a platter. Mix the last 20 ml of olive oil with the red wine vinegar, the sugar and chilli flakes. Finely chop the mint and add it to the dressing, which you can spoon over the aubergines up to an hour before serving. Sprinkle with breadcrumbs and serve.

lentil, red pepper and goat's cheese salad

250 g Puy lentils

5 large red peppers

Olive oil

Salt and pepper

Balsamic vinegar

1 red onion, peeled and finely chopped

2 celery sticks, finely chopped

2 cloves garlic, peeled and crushed

3 sprigs thyme

1 bay leaf

600 ml water

Squeeze lemon juice

Bunch flat leaf parsley

Bunch watercress

Approx. 200 g soft goat's cheese

For the dressing:

100 ml olive oil

2 tsp Dijon mustard

Squeeze honey

1 tbsp balsamic vinegar

1 tbsp sherry vinegar

This salad is vegetarian, great for you and full of your five a day. With the lentils, red peppers, onions, celery and watercress, it probably gets you up to two full portions out of your five. Bar peeling the red peppers, it's also very easy to make.

Serves 6 as a side

If you can, soak the Puy lentils in cold water for 20 minutes, as it will speed up the cooking time. Cut the peppers in half and remove the seeds. Rub lightly with some olive oil and grill until charred and black. Then put in a bowl and cover with cling film. When cool enough to handle, peel and discard the skin, slice and put back in the bowl and add a few glugs of olive oil, salt, pepper and a tiny drop of balsamic. Leave to keep warm and marinate.

Sauté the red onion, celery and garlic in some olive oil until soft but not coloured. Season well. Add in the drained lentils and mix well. Add the thyme, bay leaf and water. Season more and simmer for about 20–25 minutes until tender. Drain and cool down before mixing with lemon juice and the red peppers.

Make the salad dressing by mixing all the ingredients together and pouring over the warm lentils. Add the parsley and serve with goat's cheese crumbled on top and some watercress.

160

wild rice and sweetcorn salad

This would go nicely with any spicy meat or fish dish.

Serves 4 as a side

Approx. 150 g wild rice

1 cinnamon stick

Pinch chilli flakes

Olive oil

Salt and pepper

1 tsp Dijon mustard

Squeeze honey

3 tbsp red wine vinegar

Bunch coriander, finely chopped

1 avocado, peeled and diced

Few slices of roasted peppers from a jar or 1 red pepper, grilled and peeled

Approx. 100 g feta

Some black sesame seeds

Some basil, finely chopped

Bunch chives, finely chopped

2 ears corn on the cob, cooked and kernels removed

Cook the rice in plenty of boiling water with the cinnamon stick and some chilli. Drain and rinse until cold. Then leave to drain really well. Add a little olive oil and salt.

Mix the mustard and honey together and then slowly add in some olive oil to make a little bit of dressing. Add in the vinegar and season. Add this to the rice and check the seasoning. Then simply mix with the rest of the ingredients, adjust seasoning and serve.

161

quinoa and tomato panzanella-style salad

50 g quinoa

4 slices country-style bread (sourdough is good)

100 ml olive oil

4–8 lovely ripe tomatoes (approx. 400 g)

Good pinch caster sugar

2 cucumbers

½ red onion, very thinly diced

Mixed bunch coriander, mint and parsley, chopped

2 small cloves garlic, peeled and crushed

Juice of 1 lemon

1 tbsp red wine vinegar

Salt and pepper

Serves 4 as a side

Preheat the oven to 160°C. Cook the quinoa in boiling water for about 9 minutes. Then drain, rinse and drain again. You can cook this the night before and leave it to cool overnight (which will help to dry it out even more) and just toss with a good glug of olive oil.

Cut the bread into chunks and drizzle with olive oil and season. Bake for about 15 minutes until crisp and dry and then allow to cool.

Chop up the tomatoes and season with the sugar. Chop up the cucumbers and mix with the tomatoes, red onion, garlic and herbs. Add the lemon juice to the quinoa, season well and then mix with the tomatoes.

Whisk the red wine vinegar with the rest of the olive oil and add to the salad, mix well and adjust the seasoning.

162

leek and bread pudding

This is a good one-pot wonder vegetarian dish that would also work as part of a Sunday lunch affair instead of potatoes. It is adapted from a recipe by Thomas Keller of The French Laundry fame. It would be lovely with roast chicken.

Serves 6–8 as a side

6 really big leeks
50 g butter
Splash olive oil
Salt and pepper
3 cloves garlic, peeled and sliced
Few sprigs thyme
1 loaf decent white bread (approx. 600 g)
500 ml milk
500 ml cream
3 eggs
Grated nutmeg (optional)
250 g Gruyère or cheddar, grated

Preheat the oven to 170°C. Chop the leeks into 2–3 cm slices and then sweat them with the butter and olive oil for 10–15 minutes until good and soft in a large saucepan with a lid on it. Season really generously, add the garlic and thyme.

While this is cooking, cut the bread into 3 cm cubes and bake in the oven for 10 minutes or so until golden brown. Season the bread lightly. Beat together the milk, cream and eggs. You can grate a pinch of nutmeg to this if you like.

When the leeks are good and soft, add the toasted bread cubes, mix well and then spoon into a suitably sized gratin dish. The leeks should come quite high up the dish, but you do need to allow for the cream mixture to go in, so leave enough room.

Pour the cream mixture over the leeks and then top with grated cheese. Leave it for 15 minutes to 1 hour or so to soak before baking for about 1 hour till the top is golden brown. Allow to cool a little so the filling can settle and then serve.

jewelled couscous

200 g giant couscous
(or regular)

Zest and juice of 1 lemon

Zest and juice of 1 orange

2 tbsp red wine vinegar

3 tbsp olive oil

Salt and pepper

$^1/_2$ tsp mixed allspice

10 dried figs, roughly chopped

1 tbsp dried cherries

1 tbsp dried cranberries

1 red chilli, deseeded and finely
chopped

70 g shelled pistachio nuts

Seeds and juice of
1 pomegranate

4 spring onions, trimmed and
sliced

1 cucumber, deseeded and
sliced

Big bunch mint, parsley
and/or basil

This jewelled couscous is a bit of a mishmash of several recipes. The key to this dish is to tone down the lemon juice by adding some orange juice. Mixing in chillies, allspice and lots of dried fruit will also give it a warming feeling. Pomegranate will keep it crunchy and interesting, as will the cucumber and handfuls of chopped fresh herbs.

Serves 6–8 as a side

This couldn't be simpler. Cook the couscous according to instructions, then drain and rinse under cold water until warm. Let it cool down and drain completely. Then put it in a big bowl, pour the lemon and orange zest and juice over it, along with the red wine vinegar and olive oil. Add the allspice and season really well.

Then add in the rest of the ingredients, mix really well and taste. Adjust seasoning as desired: you may want more lemon juice or vinegar to give it more kick; you may even want a little squeeze of honey or maple syrup; or simply add more spices, including salt and pepper. Serve at room temperature.

roast aubergine with curry yoghurt

2 aubergines
About 50 ml olive oil

For the curry yoghurt:
250 g Greek yoghurt
2 cloves garlic, peeled and crushed
Juice from one lemon
2 tsp turmeric
2 tsp curry powder
Good pinch caster sugar
Salt and pepper
Big handful basil leaves (optional)
Small handful toasted pine nuts (optional)

This aubergine dish is a great side dish that will inevitably take centre-stage and would be lovely served with grilled lamb or with nice meatballs. The curry yoghurt would also be nice served with boiled, new season potatoes.

Serves 4–6 as a side

Preheat the oven to 220°C. Slice the aubergines into 2–3 cm thick rounds. Lay out on a baking tray and sprinkle generously with salt. Leave for 10–15 minutes and wipe off the water and salt from the aubergines with some paper towels.

Daub each aubergine slice with olive oil and season again with some salt and pepper. Roast in the oven for about 30 minutes until golden brown. If you want, flip them over halfway through cooking. When they're done, you can serve them warm with the yoghurt drizzled on top, or else refrigerate for up to three days and serve cold with the yoghurt.

To make the curry yoghurt, mix the yoghurt with everything except the basil and pine nuts. You can add a tablespoon of water if it's too thick. Season and drizzle over the aubergines on a platter with some basil and toasted pine nuts.

165

roast cauliflower and blue cheese salad

500 g baby potatoes
1–2 heads cauliflower
1–2 tbsp curry powder
1–2 tbsp turmeric
Salt and pepper
Olive oil
Handful sliced almonds
120–160 g blue cheese
Handful golden sultanas
Big bunch flat-leaf parsley
or coriander

Roasted cauliflower florets with olive oil, salt, pepper, turmeric and mild curry powder are a lovely and simple accompaniment to any meal. You can bulk them out by adding baby potatoes, blue cheese and some sultanas for added sweetness.

Serves 4 as a side

Preheat the oven to 190–200°C. Slice the potatoes in half or thirds. Break the cauliflower into florets. Put them into one or two roasting trays. Bear in mind they need a lot of room, so best to use two trays. Sprinkle the curry powder and turmeric on top and season well. Then drizzle a good bit of olive oil over the veg and toss around. They should be reasonably well coated. Roast for about 20–30 minutes, tossing regularly. If necessary, adjust the oven temperature and add more oil.

A few minutes before you are finished, add in the almonds so that they toast briefly. Then remove from the oven and cool down a good bit before putting in a large bowl and adding chunks of blue cheese, the sultanas and a big bunch of chopped herbs. Toss well. Serve warm rather than hot.

166

winter salad

500 g Puy lentils

Bay leaf

125 ml olive oil

6–8 raw chorizo sausages or 2 ready-to-eat chorizo sausages (about 400 g)

Approx. 250 g baby spinach

Big bunch parsley

450 g tinned artichokes, drained

1 tbsp wholegrain mustard

1 tsp honey

2 cloves garlic, peeled and crushed

50 ml sherry vinegar

Salt and pepper

200 g goat's cheese, to serve

This warm winter salad could work as a main or really delicious side salad. Puy lentils are the type of thing that could happily accompany any dish, from a nice piece of fish to a chicken or duck breast. Chorizo is one of those things that is so tasty, but often only served for special occasions.

Serves 4–6 as a side

Give the Puy lentils a good rinse and then cook in plenty of boiling water with the bay leaf and a splash of olive oil until tender. Then drain well and leave them to continue draining and stay warm while you finish off the dish.

While the lentils are cooking, cook the raw chorizo sausages by frying in a pan with a little oil to get them going or by grilling them just as you would regular sausages. Slice when done. (Or slice the ready-to-eat cooked/cured chorizo sausages and fry them in a little oil until crispy on both sides. These are my preference as they go very crispy and are full of flavour.) Drain the chorizo on kitchen paper and then put the lentils in a large bowl and mix with the chorizo slices.

Add the spinach and toss. The residual heat will wilt the spinach ever so slightly. Chop the parsley and mix in, along with the artichokes, which you can slice in half.

Mix the wholegrain mustard with the honey and garlic and then whisk in the remaining olive oil. Add the vinegar, whisk and season with some salt and black pepper. Pour the dressing over the salad, mix well and season to taste. Pile onto plates with some more leaves if you fancy it and crumble some goat's cheese on top.

index